STRANGER THINGS AND THE '80s

THE COMPLETE RETRO GUIDE

STRANGER THINGS AND THE '80s

THE COMPLETE RETRO GUIDE

JOSEPH VOGEL

CARDINAL BOOKS

Cover design by R.J.V.
Cover art: iStock/Getty Images/Etsy
Published by Cardinal Books
Distributed by Ingram Book Company

Library of Congress Cataloging-in-Publication Data
Vogel, Joseph, 1981-
Stranger Things and the '80s/ Joseph Vogel
p.   cm.

Hardback ISBN: 978-0981650616
Paperback ISBN: 978-0981650623

1. Stranger Things—Film & Television—United States
2. Stranger Things—Criticism and Interpretation
3. Stranger Things—Guides and Reviews
4. 1980s—History—Popular Culture
5. Vogel, Joseph. I. Title.

Published in the U.S.A.

1 2 3 4 5 6 7 8 9 10

Printed in the United States of America

Dedicated to Sofi and Jude,
my go-to Stranger Things *fans and fact-checkers*

CONTENTS

STRANGER THINGS AND THE '80s

Introduction

As a child of the '80s, *Stranger Things* hooked me from the opening title sequence—the eerie, glowing red letters that resembled the font on an old Stephen King novel; the moody, staticky synth theme; the VHS-like flickering of the black screen.

It hit all the right notes. It was almost like we had somehow overlooked it on some outlying movie store shelf back in 1983; but now, here it was, recovered and restored in all its analog-era glory.

As a TV series, *Stranger Things* can be classified as many things: sci-fi, horror, coming-of-age, teen drama, comedy, action-adventure. But it is, perhaps above all, a tribute to an era—as the show description puts it: "a love letter to the '80s."

That's the focus of the book in your hands. It documents how thoroughly immersed the show is in '80s culture, from its soundtrack, to its characters, to its technology, to its bikes. But I didn't just want a series of lists or trivia—there's already plenty of that online. Instead, my approach was to tell a story—or, rather, many stories—about the show's relationship with the decade in which it takes place (and takes inspiration).

So, for example, the book won't just tell you what video games are in the Palace Arcade in Season 2; it will explain how video games (and arcades) transformed youth culture in the '80s and what role they play in the show. It won't just tell you which Spielberg movies influenced the Duffer Brothers the most; it will take you inside the scenes, characters and concepts that draw from those films.

If *Stranger Things* is a love letter to the '80s, this book is your in-depth guide to the era it revives.

A Cultural Phenomenon

Stranger Things has only been around for a few years. Yet in that short time, it has generated a following as large and passionate as anything on television (or any other screen, big or small, for that matter). It is that rare crossover hit enjoyed by kids, teens, and parents alike. Its actors are now international celebrities; its characters social media sensations (see #JusticeforBarb).

In both of its first two seasons, *Stranger Things* received Golden Globe nominations for Best Television Series. It also amassed 31 Emmy nominations, including for Outstanding Drama Series. While Netflix is notoriously reticent about viewership numbers, Nielsen estimates that its Season Two premier was watched by 15.8 million American viewers in its first week alone. Many of those viewers binge-watched the entire season within days. Meanwhile, the review aggregator Rotten Tomatoes gives both the first and second seasons a 94% positive rating from critics and 91% from viewers. It is now so pervasive in popular culture that its merchandise sells in stores next to long-established blockbuster franchises like *Star Wars* and *Harry Potter*.

Yet before the summer of 2016, no one had heard of Eleven or Chief Hopper or Steve Harrington, all now household names. The Upside Down, Hawkins Laboratory and Demogorgons weren't yet part of our cultural lexicon. Beyond Winona Ryder, the show had no recognizable stars. It wasn't even promoted with a typical media blitz. There were no billboards or commercials. Just a few leaked details and an intriguing trailer.

Netflix was confident word would spread organically. They were right. Not long after it went live on Netflix on July 15th, 2016, it became a sensation. It seemed like everyone you talked to—neighbors, friends, colleagues, family members—was watching it (or wanted to). That month the *New York Times* declared it "the show of the summer." By Season Two, the show was Netflix's biggest hit, watched in over 190 countries by hundreds of millions of viewers, from the United States to China to Brazil.

Meet the Duffer Brothers

But let's back up a bit. To understand how and why *Stranger Things* struck such a chord, it's helpful to know where it came from. Among the most remarkable facts about the show is the relative youth and inexperience of its creators, Matt and Ross Duffer (now more widely known by their professional duo-designation, The Duffer Brothers). Twins from Durham, North Carolina, the Duffer Brothers were barely thirty years old when they conceptualized *Stranger Things*. Their first big breakthrough in the industry came in 2011, when Warner Bros. acquired the rights to their screenplay for *Hidden*, a little-known horror film that came out in 2015 and grossed a modest $350,000 dollars. They subsequently worked on the mystery Fox television series, *Wayward Pines*, where they were mentored by director M. Night Shyamalan.

It was around this time that they came up with the idea for *Stranger Things*—in its early broad strokes, a period-based, missing-person story featuring some supernatural elements and government conspiracies. They wrote a rough version of the pilot episode, along with a twenty-page proposal, hopeful about its prospects. No one, however, was willing to take a chance on it.

The Duffer Brothers estimate that their initial pitch was rejected by at least twenty people. The reasons varied. Some felt the show wouldn't work with kids in such prominent roles. Some suggested the story be built around Chief Hopper instead. Most simply weren't convinced the Duffer Brothers—unproven commodities in an industry averse to risk—could deliver a successful series on their own.

Then, in late 2014, the script came across Dan Cohen's desk, Vice President of 21 Laps Entertainment. Just a year earlier, Cohen said he was looking for something unusual and compelling from an up-and-coming director. "If I have one goal as a producer," he said, "it's to be the guy who gives the next Chris Nolan his *Batman*."

He accomplished that with the Duffer Brothers. Impressed with their vision for *Stranger Things*—which was then simply called *Montauk*, named after the Long Island town where *Jaws* was based— he passed the script along to director-producer (and founder of 21 Laps Entertainment) Shawn Levy.

Levy was a fortuitous match for the Duffer Brothers. A Canadian filmmaker best known for the *Night at the Museum* franchise, Levy had also recently produced the critically acclaimed 2016 sci-fi movie, *Arrival*. He was immediately intrigued by the *Montauk* script. 21 Laps, however, rarely acquired material for television. They did movies. Yet after meeting the Duffer Brothers in person, Levy was convinced it was worth making an exception.

The Duffers knew what they wanted: the '80s backdrop, the electronic soundtrack, the Stephen King-meets-Spielberg vibe, the memorable characters. Their passion and vision for the show was contagious. "Before the meeting was over," recalls Levy, "I knew I had to do what I could to shepherd it to the screen. It was this great diamond in the rough found by Dan. I fell in love with it, completely bought into the boys and felt like they were worth betting on."

In early 2015, Levy and the Duffer Brothers fine-tuned the pitch—including putting together a mashup trailer of movies that captured the feel and tone of the show. They made their first pitch to streaming juggernaut, Netflix. Having been in the industry for decades, Levy believed he understood why the Duffer Brothers' script had been overlooked to this point. As he put it: "In the movie business, unless you are a superhero, a franchise, or a fairytale, it is almost possible to get made at a studio." In the era of streaming, however, television was different. Not only was TV in the midst of a so-called "platinum era" of incredible content (*Breaking Bad, House of Cards, Orange is the New Black, Game of Thrones*); it was more open to fresh faces and ideas.

Levy believed Netflix was the perfect match for *Stranger Things*—young and agile enough to take a chance on something new, but established enough to put the necessary resources behind it. Netflix, apparently, felt the same. Within 24 hours of the pitch, they bought the series. As significantly, they agreed to give Levy and the Duffer Brothers complete creative control. "When we sold this," said Levy, "it had no pre-awareness title, no big star actor or showrunner, just these young twin brothers with a crazy idea, vividly realized, and a movie director as the producer. They really empowered us and let us lead the way."

Generation Oregon Trail

For a show so immersed in the '80s, some are surprised to learn that the Duffer Brothers were actually too young to really remember most of the decade as it unfolded. Born in 1984, they were just six years old by the time the curtains were officially drawn on the Reagan era.

Yet they have shown an uncanny ability to capture the zeitgeist—perhaps in part because the '80s still remained so ubiquitous in pop culture. The Duffers have proven particularly adept at capturing the experience of kids growing up in that era: a generation raised on bikes, videogames, and blockbuster movies.

What is this generation called that came of age in the '80s? The generation we see represented in kids like Will and Mike and Dustin and Lucas?

Often, they are mistakenly conflated with Generation X. That designation, however, generally describes those born in the mid-60s to mid-70s, meaning by the 1980s they were already in high school or college. The term Generation X was coined by author Douglas Coupland in his 1991 novel, *Generation X: Tales for an Accelerated Culture*. Soon, the term became shorthand for the disaffected, disillusioned children of Baby Boomers: a generation that experienced childhood *after* the momentous events of the '60s.

Gen-Xers were a generation who experienced most of their childhood in the 70s. They were the demographic MTV was aiming for when the network launched in 1981. Indeed, they are sometimes referred to as the MTV Generation, which also became shorthand for an era of apathetic slackers weaned on pop culture. Such characterizations, of course, are generalizations. But there is no question, as a whole, Generation X had a different outlook and sensibility than their parents—they were more skeptical (sometimes cynical); less inclined to change the world than to resist its expectations. Think of people like Quentin Tarantino (born 1963), Kurt Cobain (born 1967), Molly Ringwald (born 1968), and Winona Ryder (born 1971) and you get a good sense of various incarnations of Generation X. Or think of the older teenagers in *Stranger Things*—Steve, Nancy, Barb, Jonathan, and Billy. All would likely classify as Gen-Xers.

The generation that *followed* Generation X were children in the '80s. As a whole, they tended to be less angsty. This made sense, as the '80s, in many ways, was a great decade to be a kid. America was no longer experiencing the same "crisis of confidence" and "malaise" Jimmy Carter infamously described in the late '70s. The national mood was more optimistic, albeit with a range of underlying panics, crises, and fears.

What made the '80s great for kids though was the overall sense of freedom and possibility. It was the explosion of new music, TV shows, movies, and video games. It was all of the exciting new technologies: Macintosh Computers, Sony Walkmans, Ataris and Nintendos. It was no coincidence that most of these new technologies were geared toward kids. We were the first generation to grow up, from our earliest years, on home videos, video games, and portable music.

Strangely, this generation, which has been so frequently represented in popular culture, has often either been mischaracterized or simply gone unnamed. As journalist Anna Garvey writes: "We're an enigma, those of us born at the tail end of the '70s and the start of the '80s. Some of the 'generational' experts lazily glob us on to Generation X, and others just shove us over to the Millennials they love to hate—no one really gets us or knows where we belong. We've been called Generation Catalano, Xennials, and The Lucky Ones, but no name has really stuck for this strange micro-generation that has both a healthy portion of Gen X grunge cynicism, and a dash of the unbridled optimism of Millennials."

As remedy, Garvey proposes we be called the Oregon Trail Generation after the educational computer game featured in most American classrooms in the '80s. "If you can distinctly recall the excitement of walking into your weekly computer lab session and seeing a room full of Apple 2Es displaying the start screen of Oregon Trail," she writes, "you're a member of this nameless generation, my friend." The Oregon Trail Generation grew up on Spielberg, Michael Jackson and Mario Bros. We watched Saturday morning cartoons like *He-Man* and *Transformers*, *Alvin and the Chipmunks* and *Duck Tales*. We learned about books on *Reading Rainbow*. We grew up obsessed with franchises like *Star Wars, Indiana Jones, Back to the Future*, and *Ghostbusters*. And we rode bikes.

The kids at Hawkins Middle School—including Will, Mike, Lucas, Dustin, Eleven, and Max—are, no doubt, part of this generation. So am I—which is one of the reasons the show resonates. And even though they are on the younger outskirts, having been born in 1984, so too are the Duffer Brothers.

The '80s 2.0

There is a reason why a kid who grew up in California and a kid who grew up in Indiana or North Carolina or Colorado have similar memories of the 1980s. It is because, whatever the distinct regional and familial details of our lives, our memories are saturated with shared touchstones from popular culture. As author and journalist David Sirota explains, the '80s, for us, was not so much a historical moment as a language. "I don't remember the 1980s," he writes, "as much as I speak it and think in it." Sirota writes about how he and his brothers, in spite of all their differences, "patched together a common dialect of eighties references that served as diplomatic Morse code—bridging conflict, forging compromise, and filling uncomfortable silence."

What was this Morse code? "In [our] household," Sirota explains, "you could garner forgiveness with a proper mimic of *Planes, Trains and Automobiles* ('Sorry,' whispered like a pajama-clad Del Griffith), demand someone do something by quoting *Indiana Jones* ('Do it, now!' with a clenched fist)…describe the weather in *The Empire Strikes Back* terms ('It's like Hoth out there!'), and tell anyone to do just about anything with the generic mantra of *Rocky III* ('Go for it,' mumbled with the Italian Stallion's guttural inflection)."

We see this "secret language" all over *Stranger Things*. The kids make all kinds of pop culture allusions, from *Halloween,* to *Star Wars*, to *Ghostbusters*. These aren't just clever, ironic references. This is the way kids talked in the '80s. Moreover, we see constant visual references that recall our favorite movies from that decade; we hear the music we had in our cassette tape collections; we recognize story lines from Stephen King novels (and their film adaptations).

More than any filmmakers since those operating in the actual decade, the Duffer Brothers cracked the code of the '80s. How did they do it?

In part, it was simply a natural extension of their interests and inspirations. Once they decided to set the show in the Reagan era, they explained, it allowed them to "pay homage to all the things that inspired us most. Maybe we could catch a little bit of the feeling of Stephen King's books and the Spielberg movies. We allowed all these influences to converge into the idea for the show."

Yet their encyclopedic knowledge of the decade was never intended to feel gimmicky or obvious. It wasn't intended to be an endless litany of '80s Easter Eggs. Explains Matt Duffer:

> Sometimes I see people write about [*Stranger Things*] and they say they like that the show is "self-aware." And I guess I really didn't want it to be self-aware. We never wanted to be ironic; we didn't want to wink at the audience. We wanted it to play like one of those movies would've back then, that was sort of the goal. So the hope with the references or whatever is that they don't pull people out of it. The way we tried to get away with that was being truthful to what the characters would do in their situations and make sure it all makes sense.

The references and homages, that is, are about authenticity—not just to the period, but to the filmmakers, artists, and authors that first translated that period. In particular, *Stranger Things* is the offspring of the cinematic world of the '80s. "These are the movies that we grew up on," explained Matt Duffer, "and whether it's right or not, we prefer the way they look aesthetically and we like the way they sound. We shot on a digital camera, but we added film grain, and we wanted to have a very sort of filmic look."

This kind of attention to detail was put into every element of the show: from the way the characters dressed and talked, to their hairstyles, bedrooms, bikes, cars, and walkie talkies. But it was also about the aesthetic presentation of the show—the way it was filmed, edited and produced. "We tested quite heavily to make sure that our images had the soft and round tones that are in '80s films," explained Director of Photography Tim Ives. "Our goal [was] to make this thing feel like something that you'd lost and you hadn't seen in such a long time. You missed it in the '80s, and you were going to watch it now—a found piece. That was the desire, and that was everybody's mantra."

Modern and Nostalgic

That objective brings us back to the title sequence. The now-iconic introduction to *Stranger Things* was inspired, in part, by legendary motion graphics and titles designer Richard Greenberg. Greenberg designed a number of famous title sequences in the late 70s and '80s, including those for *Superman, Alien, Altered States, The Goonies, Dirty Dancing,* and *Die Hard*. He was known, as the Duffers explained, "for using the lettering of the movie titles to create hypnotic combinations of movement and color and shadow."

The Duffers were also inspired by the typography on many Stephen King novels from this period. According to Imaginary Forces (the design house hired to create the opening title), the brothers sent stacks of King novels to convey their vision for what the title should look like. With this guidance, more modern designs were scrapped for the more retro-looking font, ITC Benguiat, which was used on the cover of King's 1980 novel *Firestarter* (it is also featured on the Smiths' 1987 album, *Strangeways, Here We Come*).

The retro font of the main title was curved slightly, and changed from white to red. Then it was placed against a flickering black screen and put in motion so that the letters gradually came together like a puzzle. In contrast to the elaborate title sequences for shows like *Game of Thrones* or *Westworld*, it was simple.

Yet an enormous amount of care went into creating subtle effects. For example, Kodath transparencies of the title were created and backlit, similar to analog techniques used in the '80s. While it was created on a computer, they tried to capture the textures and imperfections of '80s movies: the grains and light leaks and fuzzy edges. All of these small details contributed to the psychological recognition, or nostalgia, many viewers experience when watching the opening credits.

And then there was the music. The Duffer Brothers knew they wanted an electronic soundtrack. As much as they loved Spielberg, they felt the show demanded something different sonically—something closer to the music of John Carpenter, Vangelis, Tangerine Dream, or Giorgio Moroder. To test out this impulse, they put together a mock trailer of '80s movies overlaid with John Carpenter music. "As soon as we heard John Carpenter's eerie synth drones play over shots from *E.T.*, we got major goosebumps. It worked, big time." For *Stranger Things*, the Duffers were looking for something similarly moody and synthy—something that "would feel both modern and nostalgic at the same time."

They found what they were looking for in Austin-based synth band, SURVIVE. Comprised of two members, Michael Stein and Kyle Dixon, SURVIVE was not well-known outside the indie electronic scene prior to *Stranger Things*. They built a following through their use of analog synthesizers, rather than more typical Pro Tools-based electronic music. Consequently, their sound and feel hearkened back to the late 70s and '80s, when analog synthesizers were in their prime. The Duffer Brothers learned of the group through their contributions to the 2014 horror thriller, *The Guest*. That film wasn't widely known, but its retro vibe spoke to the Duffers.

A demo by SURVIVE called "Prophecy" ended up evolving into the title theme. The signature bass line was created on a Roland SH-2, a popular synthesizer that allows you to create rich harmonics. They filtered the sound to ebb and flow in volume, gradually building in intensity. They used the Prophet V, another popular synth in the late '70s and '80s, for the bedding. This was the synthesizer used in many John Carpenter movies.

Then they added details: the arpeggio-like sparkling at the very beginning; the heartbeat-like drumbeat, which adds a sense of foreboding and suspense; and the electric buzzing sound effects. All of this was choreographed to sync with the title sequence. The final product was exactly what the Duffer Brothers wanted: something dark, but warm; familiar, but mysterious. Its moody, minimalist pulse perfectly captured the feel of the show.

It is this attention to detail—to fonts, sounds, styles, and effects—that makes *Stranger Things* special. It is what makes the show seem like it is not just set in the '80s, but from the '80s—as if the Duffers somehow captured the era in a bottle.

A Curiosity Voyage

The chapters that follow explore *Stranger Things'* relationship to the '80s through eleven different entry points: Stephen King, Spielberg, '80s Movies, '80s Music, Childhood, The Reagan Era, Playing Games, Science and Technology, Food and Fashion, The Outsiders, and A Hero's Journey. While it is intended to be read from beginning to end, it is also amenable to jumping around.

For example, if you're itching to learn more about The Clash's 1982 song, "Should I Stay or Should I Go?" head over to Chapter 4. If you want to understand how the show is connected to John Hughes' legendary teen films (*The Breakfast Club*, *Ferris Bueller*, etc.) turn to Chapter 3. If you want to know the significance of Eggo waffles, turn to Chapter 9. And if you want to know which Stephen King novel was most influential to the Duffer Brothers, well, you're almost there—turn to Chapter 1.

I settled on the number of chapters (eleven) in honor of, yep, *her*: the iconic character performed by Millie Bobby Brown. Chapter 11 focuses primarily on her cultural significance as well as her "hero's journey" in the show.

Be aware from the outset: spoilers abound throughout the book. It is intended to be read *after* watching the show.

There is no doubt that part of *Stranger Things'* appeal has to do with nostalgia—people love to revisit the past and the '80s, for a variety of reasons, have proven particularly captivating. In a 2018 article, *Newsweek* asked, "Why Do We Love the '80s So Much?" pointing not only to the *Stranger Things* phenomenon, but also to movies like *Ready Player One*, albums like Taylor Swift's *1989*, and a revival of '80s styles and fashions.

Often overlooked is that this revival has been, in large part, driven by young people. That's what has made *Stranger Things* such a phenomenon. Many of the the show's most ardent fans never lived through the '80s. It is just as popular, if not more, among Millenials and Gen-Zers as it is for Gen-Xers and Oregon Trail-ers. Young fans are fascinated by the history inside the story: they want to know more about The Clash, Stephen King, and *Ghostbusters*; they are enamored with the bikes, walkie talkies, and latchkey freedom.

That's what this book is about—all those period details, connections, references, and inspirations that make the show what it is. Dustin would call it a "curiosity voyage."

So…whether you lived through the '80s or not, this book is your Delorean, and we're headed back to the Reagan era. Very few shows encourage that kind of journey more than *Stranger Things*.

1

Stephen King

In July of 2016, bestselling author Stephen King tweeted that watching *Stranger Things* was like watching a mashup of his own greatest hits. "I mean that in a good way," he clarified. He wasn't wrong.

Fans of the horror writer have documented in exhaustive detail connections—both subtle and explicit—between his work and *Stranger Things*. For their part, the Duffer Brothers have gratefully acknowledged this influence in nearly every interview they have given about the show. "Growing up he was such an inspiration," Ross Duffer told *The Hollywood Reporter*. "—he's like a god to us, and so, it's been surreal just communicating with him at all." Part of what *Stranger Things* has reminded viewers is Stephen King's outsized influence—not just on the Duffers, but on the 1980s more broadly.

In that decade, King was a cultural phenomenon. His novels were ubiquitous in grocery stores, malls, and night stands. In terms of sheer book sales, he was in a league of his own, selling an estimated 100 million copies over the course of the decade. In 1987, four of his novels appeared on the *New York Times* bestseller at the same time, something that had never happened before.

According to *Publisher Weekly*, of the twenty five bestselling books of the decade, seven were written by King.

In a *Time* cover story on the author in 1986, King described himself as "the literary equivalent of a Big Mac and large fries from McDonald's." King's remark effectively captured his widespread appeal to ordinary people. However, it also highlighted a common criticism—that his work was cheap, formulaic and frivolous "genre fiction" (literary critic Harold Bloom infamously dismissed him as "another low in the shocking process of dumbing down our cultural life").

Yet regardless of such snobbish criticisms, King's novels resonated—not only because they spoke so intimately to readers, but also because they spoke so directly to the period in which they were released. King's work was about what was beneath the placid surface—the nightmare beneath the American Dream. He wrote about religious fanaticism, government conspiracies, drug and alcohol abuse, discrimination, bullying, and social panics. His work explored our fears, anxieties, secrets, and sins. His characters were often outsiders, freaks, losers, and loners.

When someone bought (or checked out) a Stephen King book, they knew they were getting a story guaranteed to entertain—and usually to terrify. Clearly, that formula struck a chord in the '80s. Not only were they massively popular novels, many were also adapted into iconic movies, including:

- *The Shining* (novel published in 1977; movie released in 1980)
- *The Dead Zone* (novel published in 1979; movie released in 1983)
- *Firestarter* (novel published in 1980; movie released in 1984)
- *Cujo* (novel published in 1981; movie released in 1983)
- *The Running Man* (novel, published under the pseudonym Richard Bachman, in 1982; movie released in 1987)

- *The Body* (novella published in the collection *Different Seasons* in 1982; movie, *Stand By Me*, released in 1986)
- *Rita Hayworth and Shawshank Redemption* (novella published in the collection *Different Seasons* in 1982; movie, *The Shawshank Redemption*, released in 1994)
- *Pet Sematary* (novel published in 1983; movie released in 1989)
- *It* (novel published in 1986; made-for-TV-movie released in 1990; feature film released in 2017)
- *Misery* (novel published in 1987; movie released in 1990)

King's prolific output in this period—and its cultural saturation through both books and movies—is probably unparalleled. As author Tony Magistrale puts it: "What the Beatles were to rock music in the 1960s, Stephen King was to horror fiction and film in the 1980s."

Stand By Me

How does King's influence manifest in *Stranger Things*? As mentioned in the Introduction, the connection begins in the opening title sequence. That blood red retro type is the exact same font—ITC Benguiat—used on many Stephen King novels in the '80s, including *Firestarter*. Moreover, the mood it establishes taps into the dark, foreboding feel of King's work.

The connection becomes even clearer in Chapter 4, Season 1 ("The Body"). The title of the episode is an homage to the short story of the same name by King, included in his 1982 collection, *Different Seasons*. That story is better known as the source material for the classic 1986 film, *Stand By Me*, directed by Rob Reiner and featuring standout performances from Wil Wheaton (Gordie), River Phoenix (Chris), Corey Feldman (Teddy), and Jerry O'Connell (Vern). The movie is widely recognized as one of the best coming-of-age films of all time.

Even Stephen King has praised it as his favorite adaptation of his work. "I thought it was true to the book," he explained, "...it had the emotional gradient of the story. It was moving... When the movie was over, I hugged [director Rob Reiner] because I was moved to tears, because it was so autobiographical."

Ross Duffer describes *Stand By Me* as the "pinnacle of child performances in movies or shows," an authenticity he wanted to replicate in *Stranger Things*. Indeed, the Duffers admired the performances so much that, when casting for the show, they actually had the kids recite lines from the movie for their auditions.

That decision makes a lot of sense given how much *Stranger Things* depended on casting child actors who, as in *Stand By Me*, felt fully inhabited and real. Moreover, both stories capture a similar moment in life. Like *Stand By Me*, *Stranger Things* features four young kids who embark on a journey together. That journey, at times treacherous, at times funny, at times profoundly moving, not only allows them to grow as individuals, it also solidifies their bond as friends.

A number of scenes in *Stranger Things* draw direct inspiration from *Stand By Me*. Anyone familiar with the movie immediately recognized the visual in Season 1, Chapter 5 ("The Flea and the Acrobat") when the kids are walking along the train tracks. It almost identically mirrors the iconic railroad trek in *Stand By Me*—only instead of four boys, Eleven (played by Millie Bobby Brown) is part of the crew, walking alongside Mike (played by Finn Wolfhard), as Lucas (played by Caleb McLaughlin) walks next to Dustin (played by Gaten Matarazzo). The Duffers have acknowledged the *Stand By Me* inspiration for the scene (which is revisited in Season 2, this time with Steve (played by Joe Keery) and Dustin walking the tracks).

Not only do these scenes look beautiful on camera; they symbolize the kids' journey. They also represent a crossroads, suggesting the characters will end up in a different place than where they started. Perhaps most importantly, the train track scenes allow *Stranger Things* to do what *Stand By Me* did so well—capture the vulnerability and camaraderie of the characters. Here, away from school and home and the town, they can be truly honest with each other.

As in *Stand By Me*, the kids in *Stranger Things* are searching for something—literally and figuratively. In *Stand By Me* it is literally a dead body; in *Stranger Things*, their lost, but—they hope—still living friend, Will (played by Noah Schnapp). What they are searching for figuratively is more complex: an escape, an adventure, a connection, understanding. What both stories so well is capture the intimacy of childhood friendship. As the narrator from *Stand By Me* famously reflects: "I never had any friends later on like the ones I had when I was twelve. Jesus, does anyone?"

Like *Stand By Me*, friendship is central to *Stranger Things*. It is so important to the boys they feel compelled to explain what it means to Eleven, who has never had friends before. Friends keep their promises, they tell her. Friends don't lie. Friends have each other's backs. Eleven is eventually accepted into the group for doing just those things.

We see a number of instances of her loyalty throughout Season 1. In Chapter 6 ("The Monster"), for example, Dustin and Mike are ambushed by their arch-enemies, Troy and James. Troy puts a knife to Dustin's throat, threatening to cut his teeth out if Mike doesn't jump off the cliff into the lake below. The scene closely resembles a scene from *Stand By Me*, in which the boys finally discover the missing body, only to be confronted by Ace Merrill and his gang.

Like Troy with Dustin, Ace pulls a switchblade on Chris. In both scenes, however, the threatened boys escape—in *Stand By Me* when Gordie unexpectedly pulls a gun out to save his friend Chris, and in *Stranger Things* through the supernatural heroics of Eleven, who first rescues Mike mid-air from his fall off the cliff, and then breaks Troy's arm with her mind. Both scenes are dramatic moments in their respective stories; however, they also demonstrate the importance of true friends.

The Duffers knew they wanted to capture the magic of *Stand By Me* (and its source story, "The Body") in *Stranger Things*: a coming-of-age story that is suspenseful and scary, but also emotionally moving. "We love that story and that film with all of our boyish hearts, and its DNA is written all over the show," they acknowledged.

The feeling, apparently, is mutual. Not only has Stephen King expressed admiration for the series; Wil Wheaton, who played Gordie in *Stand By Me*, had high praise for *Stranger Things*, calling it "one of the greatest things I've ever experienced in my life as an audience member." As with *Stand By Me*, he attributes much of its resonance to the characters. "It's what makes something like *Stranger Things* so wonderful and so rewarding and so memorable. We get to see actors who we've never seen before just become these roles. We can embrace the characters and they become real the same way the characters in *Stand by Me* did for our generation."

IT

Just as deeply woven into the DNA of *Stranger Things* is another Stephen King classic: the sprawling, 1,200-page novel, *It*. Originally released in 1986, *It* quickly became a sensation, selling over 800,000 copies in its first run and spending fourteen weeks at the top of the *New York Times* bestseller list. In spite of its flaws, it is now widely considered one of King's best novels.

Asked by the *Hollywood Reporter*, which of all of Stephen King's books was most formative for them, both Duffer brothers selected *It*. "It's the big one," confirmed Ross, "and *It* is obviously a huge inspiration for the show. That's probably the biggest [influence], I think just because we're the age of those characters when we're reading it, so it's not that his other books aren't amazing, they were." Matt concurred: "That made probably the biggest impact on us...I re-read *It* again, it's been like five or six years, but it's such an incredible book."

Like *Stand By Me*, *It* is about a group of misfit friends—they call themselves "The Losers Club"—who are bound together by grappling with trauma and confronting both internal and external terrors. That terror and trauma comes from a number of sources. There is the Bowers Gang—a group of bullies led by the sadistic and sociopathic Henry Bowers. A close corollary to Henry in *Stranger Things* is Billy (played by Dacre Montgomery): a similarly abusive, racist, homophobic "human antagonist," who, like Henry, has a history of being abused himself.

And then there is It, the mysterious, demonic, shape-shifting creature that takes the form of each child's greatest fear. Its most common form, of course, is as the clown, Pennywise—one of the most iconic villains of all time. Pennywise famously lures George into the sewer, from which the young boy never returns. But his appetite for children stretches long before and beyond that terrifying incident in 1957. A primordial being, he returns to haunt and prey on the young of Derry, Maine every 27 years.

In *Stranger Things*, the kids also encounter a mysterious, supernatural creature that preys on humans. Like It, this creature is nameless until the boys, drawing from Dungeons & Dragons, decide to name it the Demogorgon. Like It, the Demogorgon is a mostly subterranean creature, emerging from another dimension: the Upside Down. And like It, the Demogorgon is as terrifying as it is deadly. Confronting this primal source of fear and terror, as in It, becomes the central conflict of Season 1 of *Stranger Things* (in Season 2, the primary villain becomes the larger, cosmic evil of the Mind Flayer).

Beyond these larger conceptual similarities, there are a number of more specific allusions to *It* in *Stranger Things*. In Season 1, Chapter 1 ("The Vanishing of Will Byers"), we see a flashback in which Joyce surprises Will with tickets to see the 1983 horror movie, *Poltergeist*. Will assures his mom that he'll be fine watching the movie, that he doesn't get scared anymore, to which she replies, "Oh yeah? Not even of... clowns?" —a clear reference to Pennywise (even though the novel technically wasn't published for another few years).

In Season 2, Chapter 3 ("The Pollywog"), clowns come up again. This time Will is talking with Bob Newby (played by Sean Astin), who volunteered to drive him to school. Empathetic about Will's still-lingering trauma from the events of the previous year, Bob tells Will about an experience he had as a child, in which he was waiting in line at a fair when he was tapped on the shoulder by a clown named Mr. Baldo. "Hey kiddo, would you like a balloon?" the clown said. The line is almost identical to a line in the film adaptation of *It* when Pennywise asks George, "Do you want a balloon?" before luring him into the sewer.

After Season 2 premiered, *Stranger Things* fans took the connection a step further. Bob Newby, fans noted, was from Maine, and would have been a kid in the late 1950s: the exact location and time frame of the events in *It*. Was it possible that these two fictional worlds were colliding? Was Bob literally one of the boys from *It*? The Duffer Brothers didn't confirm or dismiss the theory.

In an interview with *Vulture*, however, Matt Duffer did acknowledge that, like Bob, he and his brother had a major fear of clowns—in large part because of *It*. "It was a real problem for me," he said. "Then in 1990, we saw the *It* mini-series and Tim Curry's performance as Pennywise *really* messed me up. Like, it scarred me in a major way. It was one of the first true horror things I had seen, and I had not experienced Stephen King before. That was my first experience with Stephen King, so that was a really huge point in my life. It was two weeks, at least, of no sleep because of that. So yeah, I think [Bob's clown story] was really me describing something that just freaked me out. I didn't have that experience myself. I just had nightmares like that."

Whether Bob is literally from the fictional world of *It* is left up to the audience, but Matt Duffer does concede that "Stephen King exists in this world."

Yet another connection to *It* is Lucas's use of a slingshot. Dustin repeatedly mocks Lucas for thinking he can take on a Demogorgon with such an inferior weapon. The slingshot, however, carries a mythical association as the weapon of the underdog. It was the weapon David used to defeat Goliath. It features in precisely this context in the 1990 adaptation of *It*, in which Pennywise is finally taken down by a child with a slingshot. Similarly, in *Stranger Things*, Lucas breaks out the slingshot in the climactic showdown with the Demogorgon in Season 1, Chapter 8 ("The Upside Down"). While the first few shots barely impact the monster, the final shot goes straight in the head, blasting the monster back against the classroom chalkboard, where Eleven effectively finishes the job.

So great was their interest in *It*, the Duffer Brothers actually pitched Warner Bros to direct the 2017 film adaptation of the novel (this was back in 2014 before *Stranger Things*). Since it was such a sprawling novel, their idea was to tackle it an an eight to ten hour series. Ultimately, however, the movie was handed over to the more established director, Andy Muschietti. His 2017 translation of the novel was a massive success, becoming the highest-grossing horror movie of all time. Ironically, it also featured one of the main actors from *Stranger Things*: Finn Wolfhard (Mike), who plays Richie in *It*.

Read Any Stephen King?

Beyond the big two—*Stand By Me* and *It*—there are a number of other Stephen King references in *Stranger Things*. When Chief Hopper (played by David Harbour) and Joyce (played by Winona Ryder) visit Terry Ives in Season 1, Chapter 6 ("The Monster"), her sister Becky explains that Terry believed her child (Jane) was stolen from her because of her "special abilities." Joyce asks what she means by special abilities. "Read any Stephen King?" Becky says. "Telepathy, telekinesis...you know, shit you can do with your mind." The scene ends, not coincidentally, with a clown mobil spinning ominously over the crib of the missing child.

The "read any Stephen King?" line refers most obviously to two classic novels by the author about girls with supernatural abilities: *Carrie* and *Firestarter*. Published in 1974, *Carrie* is about a high school girl who is bullied and tormented by her peers until she is finally pushed too far and exacts revenge with her telekinetic powers.

Carrie was Stephen King's first published novel. It is also one of his most controversial, still frequently banned in many American schools. For King, however, the novel dealt with important subject matter: "*Carrie* is largely about how women find their own channels of power, and what men fear about women and women's sexuality," he reflected "For me, Carrie White is a sadly misused teenager, an example of the sort of person whose spirit is so often broken for good in that pit of man-and woman-eaters that is your normal suburban high school. But she's also Woman, feeling her powers for the first time and, like Samson, pulling down the temple on everyone in sight...Carrie uses her 'wild talent' to pull down the whole rotten society."

King's novel was adapted into a film by Brian de Palma, starring Sissy Spacek, in 1976, which became a cult-classic in its own right. Many viewers noted the moment when Nancy's hand reaches out of the portal in the tree in Season 1, Chapter 5 ("The Monster") closely resembled the iconic final scene from *Carrie*.

The more significant connection to *Carrie*, of course, is between their female protagonists, Carrie and Eleven—from the abuse they both suffer (Carrie in her high school, Eleven at Hawkins Lab), to their isolation and loneliness, to the gradual realization of their powers. While Eleven is ultimately less destructive, like Carrie, she can be pushed past her breaking point. She does, after all, kill several people over the first two seasons—and injure numerous others.

Perhaps even more influential on *Stranger Things* is *Firestarter*. *Firestarter* was published in 1980, and adapted into a movie—starring Drew Barrymore—in 1984. Like *Stranger Things*, *Firestarter* features a sinister government agency—referred to as The Shop—that uses human subjects for drug-induced experiments. In King's novel, the young female protagonist—Charlie McGee—also possesses a special ability: pyrokinesis—the ability to create fire with her mind. Charlie's parents also have special abilities: her mother Victoria has telekinesis and her father Andy has an auto-hypnotic power referred to as "the push." These abilities, as in *Stranger Things*, are tested and exploited by the government until Andy and Charlie manage to escape.

Like Eleven, Charlie's abilities gradually become stronger and stronger. And like Eleven, she is forced to put those powers to use, as government agents relentlessly pursue her. Both characters, in essence, are freakish fugitives, who must hide, evade, and fend off those who intend to use and control them. If the connection between the stories wasn't already uncanny enough, in the Mark Lester-directed film adaptation of *Firestarter* Charlie's father Andy, like Eleven, bleeds from his nose when using his power.

I Love That Book

Want some more Stephen King connections? How about the reference to Steve Harrington as "King Steve," a clever inversion of the author's name? Or the title of Season 1, Chapter 2— "The Weirdo on Maple Street"—which not only recalls the classic *Twilight Zone* episode, "The Monsters are Due on Maple Street," but also the 1993 short story by King, "The House on Maple Street." When Joyce chops through the exterior wall of her house with an axe in Season 1, Chapter 3 ("Holly, Jolly") many viewers recognized the similarity to the iconic scene from Stanley Kubrick's *The Shining*—based on King's 1977 novel—when Jack axes through the bathroom door, shouting, "Here's Johnny!" Ross Duffer also acknowledged that some of the wide-angle shots in the school hallways were inspired by *The Shining*.

Stephen King's response to the vast array of allusions and homages to his work in *Stranger Things* has been refreshingly gracious. After watching Season 1, he tweeted: "STRANGER THINGS is pure fun. A+. Don't miss it. Winona Ryder shines." Likewise, after watching the second season, he tweeted his approval: "STRANGER THINGS 2: Ladies and gentlemen, that's how you do it: no bullshit, balls to the wall entertainment. Straight up."

The creators of the show were understandably relieved and honored to receive such praise from their childhood hero. "He's amazing," said Matt Duffer, "and when he tweeted about *Stranger Things*, I was trying not to cry, because that was right before the premiere…It was like 20 minutes before we were supposed to get in the car, and I'm like, 'I'm barely functional right now.'"

The Duffers clearly try to pay tribute to the man from whom they drew such inspiration. Perhaps the best Stephen King nod in the series comes in Season 1, Chapter 4 ("The Body")—the episode noted earlier for sharing its title with King's classic short story. Chief Hopper arrives at the morgue to check on what may or may not be Will's body. When he arrives, a security guard is sitting on a chair, intently reading a book—which turns out to be a Stephen King novel.

On the back cover we see a picture of the author. We don't see the front. But as Chief Hopper rushes by, he gives a knowing smile, before remarking, "I love that book...That's a nasty mutt." The reference is to *Cujo*, the classic King novel about a rabid dog, which came out in 1981, and was adapted into a movie in 1983, the same year the first season of *Stranger Things* takes place. It is an appropriate recognition for the most influential author on the series and the most popular author of the '80s.

2

——————

Spielberg

If anyone was as significant to '80s culture as Stephen King, it was legendary filmmaker Steven Spielberg. In fact, the two share a lot in common: both are around the same age; both shot into the stratosphere in the mid-70s with revolutionary "genre" tales (*Carrie* and *Jaws*); and both have similar thematic preoccupations— childhood, outsiders, mystery, wonder.

"I don't know how Stephen King and I aren't related by blood," Spielberg told *Entertainment Weekly* in a 2018 interview. "I cannot believe that part of Stephen King is not Jewish, and I can't believe that we haven't actually made a movie together. I really think Stephen and I have a spiritual connection in terms of the movies and the stories we love to tell."

The pair almost teamed up for *Poltergeist* in 1982, but scheduling conflicts prevented the collaboration from coming to fruition. Their careers, however, surged through the Reagan years in parallel streams. Like King, it is impossible to imagine the '80s without Spielberg. For kids growing up in the decade, his movies were planted deep in our collective consciousness. They gave us a shared set of archetypes, symbols, characters, stories. They gave us a common language.

Spielberg was undoubtedly the most influential visual storyteller of a generation. Some critics felt his movies were juvenile, sentimental, and overblown. They identified him—and *Star Wars* creator George Lucas—as the primary culprits for a general dumbing down and softening of content in movies and an escalation of spectacle, excess, and blockbuster commodification. Spielberg's films were sometimes disparagingly referred to as "popcorn movies"—code for cheap escapism aimed at the coarse tastes of the masses.

But for most moviegoers, the consensus was different. His films were packed with wonder, magic, adventure. How could you not be swept in to *Close Encounters, Jaws, E.T.,* and *Indiana Jones*? They were pure cinematic euphoria. They represented a kind of threshold: between childhood and adulthood, between innocence and experience, between the known and unknown, between fear and transcendence. Once you entered Spielberg's universe, you were never the same.

This was certainly the experience of the Duffer Brothers. Not only did they grow up on Spielberg's movies; they became students of his craft—obsessed with how the magic on the screen was created.

They wanted that "Amblin DNA," as they described it, in *Stranger Things*. Ross Duffer explains, "What Spielberg did in the '80s was he took these kind of B-movie ideas, like flying saucers or killer sharks, and he elevated it. In this new medium, [our idea was], can we go back and try and do a little of what he did, take something that's been relegated to being cheesy, and can you do an elevated version of that?" Director of Photography Tim Ives said the mantra on the set of the first season was: "What would Spielberg do?"

E.T.

It is clear that mantra was taken to heart. No single director is as integral to the world of *Stranger Things* as Steven Spielberg. And no single movie is as important to the series as *E.T.: The Extra Terrestrial.*

Released in the summer of 1982, *E.T.* was an unusual movie to become a blockbuster, let alone the highest grossing film of all time to that point. While Spielberg directed it, it was written and produced by women (Melissa Mathison and Kathleen Kennedy, respectively), a rarity in the industry. It featured no major movie stars. And it was made on a relatively small budget—$10 million dollars (for context, the 1978 movie, *Superman*, starring Christopher Reeve, cost $55 million).

But the movie about a lonely boy befriending an unusual alien struck a chord. It became the most commercially successful movie of the decade, making over $400 million dollars—more than *Star Wars: Empire Strikes Back, Indiana Jones, Back to the Future, Batman,* or *Ghostbusters*. More than a movie, it was a cultural phenomenon. It was screened for President Reagan at the White House. Pop star Michael Jackson was so obsessed with it he agreed to narrate the audiobook. By the mid-1980s, it was part of just about every family's VHS collection.

The influence of *E.T.* on *Stranger Things* cannot be overstated. It surfaces over and over, from specific scenes and characters to broader concepts and themes. Both stories take place in small, suburban towns (*E.T.* in an unnamed suburb in California, *Stranger Things* in the fictional Hawkins, Indiana), bordered by dense, mysterious forests; both feature single mothers and latchkey kids; both, as mentioned in Chapter 1, feature bikes as symbols of childhood mobility and freedom; and both explore how society—and individuals—respond to strange, supernatural beings and events.

We see parallels to Spielberg's film immediately. The opening establishing shot of the stars, which gradually pans down to earth, is almost identical to the beginning of *E.T.* So is the first scene with the boys—Mike, Will, Lucas, and Dustin—in the Wheelers' basement. Just like *E.T.*, the setting is a suburban house at night; the kids are bantering around a table and playing the same game as the characters in *E.T.*—Dungeons & Dragons. And in both cases the food of choice is pizza (Elliot famously goes outside to retrieve it from the delivery boy, while Dustin offers a slice to Nancy—played by Natalia Dyer—on his way out).

Beyond these parallels, the Duffers wanted to capture the natural chemistry from the scene in *E.T.*: the feel of kids just being kids, not over-scripted performances for the camera. It was the first scene they wrote for the show, and they were understandably nervous about how it would translate. "We held our breath, called action, and...it clicked," they recalled. "Our boys flew through the scene effortlessly and energetically, and their chemistry was electric; they felt like they had known each other their whole lives. Other than when we sold the show to Netflix, this was the single biggest moment for *Stranger Things*."

The homages continue throughout the first chapter of Season 1 ("The Vanishing of Will Byers"). Later in the episode, when Will is fleeing from the Demogorgon, he runs outside to a nearby shed. The shed is also where Elliot first discovers E.T. The dynamics of these two scenes, however, are essentially reversed. As director of photography Tim Ives explains: "In *E.T.*, Elliot goes to the woodshed when he's looking to find the monster. Will is looking to get away from the monster and hide."

Some of the visuals in the shed scenes are also very similar. "There was a shot, very similar, that was an homage [to *E.T.*]," acknowledges Ives. "It was very wide, looking back at the house on the left and the shed on the right. It was sort of a signature shot for us that I think the audience responded quite well to."

There is no direct corollary for Elliot—the sensitive outsider—in *Stranger Things*, though we see similar qualities in both Will and Mike. Similarly, there is no direct corollary to E.T.—the loveable, wide-eyed extraterrestrial from a faraway planet. However, there are some pretty obvious connections between E.T. and Eleven.

The moment at the end of Chapter 1 ("The Vanishing of Will Byers") when the boys discover Eleven in the woods, for example, is very similar to Elliot's discovery of E.T. in the corn stalks. In both scenes, the kids carry flashlights and the encounter elicits a mutual shock. They don't know what to make of each other. E.T.'s visceral fear is replicated by Eleven, who trembles under the harsh glare of the light and rain. Like E.T., she is homeless and scared.

There are also many similarities between the relationships of Mike and Eleven and Elliot and E.T. Just as Elliot brings E.T. into his home, the boys bring Eleven back to the Wheeler house. While the other boys remain suspicious and resentful of Eleven's presence, Mike is caring and tender with her—a dynamic that closely resembles the relationship between Elliot and E.T. Somehow, they just connect.

Like Elliot, Mike acts as a kind of protector. He finds Eleven clothes and builds her a makeshift bedroom in the basement. At the beginning of Chapter 2 ("The Weirdo on Maple Street"), he brings her down Eggo waffles before leaving to school. The Duffer Brothers acknowledge "many not-so-subtle nods to *E.T.* in this chapter," particularly with the relationship between Mike and Eleven: "Just as *E.T.* is about the connection between *E.T.* and Elliot, this chapter is about the connection between Eleven and Mike. Over the course of the day, they begin to bond and empathize with one another in surprising ways." Many of those ways are wordless and intuitive, since Eleven, like E.T., barely speaks and doesn't really understand the new world she finds herself in. As the Duffer Brothers explain, she "becomes the quintessential stranger in a strange land, unfamiliar with our customs and lifestyle."

With Mike at school, Eleven—just like E.T.—is alone in the house, where she putters around and explores—eating junk food, testing out the recliner, trying to work the phone. While she doesn't get drunk like E.T., they are both mesmerized by the TV.

Like E.T., Eleven also makes things levitate with her mind: just as E.T. picks up a bunch of playdough balls and makes them rotate like the solar system, Eleven stuns the boys by making a toy Millenium Falcon rise in the air. She subsequently demonstrates much greater powers, including the ability, similar to E.T., to communicate across dimensions.

Perhaps the most widely noted connection between E.T. and Eleven comes in Season 1, Chapter 4 ("The Body"), when the boys help dress her up to go to school, including having her wear a blonde wig. E.T., of course, is similarly dressed up by Gertie, who also gives the alien a wig and dress.

In another Gertie-E.T. scene, the young girl teaches the alien—with the help of the TV—the alphabet. When E.T. says "B," Gertie responds, "Good!" which E.T. hears as "Be good!" A similar moment happens in *Stranger Things* after the boys help dress Eleven up. Mike tells her she looks pretty—but then, embarrassed, adds: *good*. Pretty good. Looking at herself in the mirror, Eleven repeats the line: "pretty...good."

While Eleven and E.T. share much in common, however, the Duffers are quick to highlight distinctions. Beyond the obvious fact that El is literally a girl (albeit a girl with supernatural abilities) and E.T. is an alien, El is also more volatile and dangerous. "Eleven isn't a normal girl," explain the Duffers, "and she's no gentle plant-collecting alien either. She has unpredictable supernatural powers that will most definitely put our boys in jeopardy."

There are numerous other nods to *E.T.* in *Stranger Things*: the parents' obliviousness to the presence of Eleven—even when living in the same house; Mike, like Elliot, faking sick to stay home from school; Dustin using a trail of bologna to lure Dart (similar to Elliot luring E.T. with a trail of Reese's Pieces). In Season 2, Chapter 4 ("Will the Wise"), as the boys discuss the possibility of Will interacting with another dimension, Mike declares: "This isn't D&D. This is real life." The line recalls Elliot's famous quip in response to the suggestion that E.T. simply "beam up" to his home planet: "This is reality, Greg!"

Then there are the recurring visuals of adults searching the forest with flashlights; of men in Hazmat suits; of the ominous presence of federal agents; of epic bike chase scenes. We even see an E.T. toy figure in Dustin's room!

More than any single film, *E.T.* is woven into the tapestry of *Stranger Things*—yet to the show's credit, it does so in a way that feels fresh and new. Eleven is like E.T., but distinct in crucial ways; Mike is like Elliot, but different; Joyce is far more fleshed out than Dee Wallace, the single mother in *E.T.* In fact, as much as *E.T.* deserves its status as an all-time classic, *Stranger Things* goes much broader and deeper in terms of character and plot development. Moreover, while *Stranger Things* certainly has its heartwarming moments, its tone is notably darker. In this way, it also resembles another Spielberg classic: *Jaws*.

Jaws

The Duffer Brothers were so inspired by *Jaws*, they almost set *Stranger Things* in the same Long Island town of Montauk (the fictional town, Amity, was based on Montauk, where a 4,500 pound great white shark was caught in the 1960s, though the movie was actually filmed on Martha's Vineyard).

"We liked Montauk," explained Matt Duffer, "because we liked the coastal setting, and Montauk was the basis for Amity, and *Jaws* is probably our favorite movie, so I thought that that would be really cool. Then it was really going to be impossible to shoot in or around Long Island in the wintertime. It was just going to be miserable and expensive." The Duffer Brothers ended up shooting *Stranger Things* in the suburbs of Atlanta, but the *Jaws* influence remains pervasive.

Jaws was released in the summer of 1975, yet it still remained in wide circulation in the '80s, during which time multiple sequels were released. Credited as the first summer blockbuster, *Jaws* was accompanied by a massive marketing and merchandise blitz, including T-shirts, books, toys, and posters. It is no surprise then that we see the iconic poster hanging in Will Byers' bedroom. *Jaws* was the highest grossing film of all time until it was surpassed by *Star Wars* (and later *E.T.*) and set the blueprint for a new generation of blockbuster movies.

Perhaps the first obvious connection to *Jaws* in *Stranger Things* comes in Season 1, Chapter 1 ("The Vanishing of Will Byers"), when we are introduced to Chief Jim Hopper and the Hawkins Police Department. Chief Hopper is a character very much in the same vein as Chief Martin Brody from *Jaws* —both former "big city" policemen with complicated pasts, now serving as police chiefs in sleepy towns.

When he first arrives at the police station, Chief Hopper's secretary informs him that "some kids are stealing some gomes" out of a local resident's garden, an incident that closely parallels an early scene in Jaws, when Chief Brody's secretary informs him that some "nine year olds from the school have been karateing the picket fences."

Both humorous anecdotes are meant to emphasize the low stakes of typical daily events in these small towns. And in both cases, another typical day in the office is suddenly disrupted with much more serious incidents: in *Jaws*, a call from the medical examiner about a girl found dead on the beach, and in *Stranger Things*, a visit from Joyce Byers, who is frantic about the disappearance of her son, Will. The Duffer Brothers acknowledged that the frame where Chief Hopper types "missing" on the police report was directly inspired by the frame in *Jaws* when Chief Brody types "shark attack."

Chief Hopper is certainly not an exact replica of Chief Brody. Hopper is more broken—we learn that his daughter, Sarah, passed away at a young age from cancer and that his marriage subsequently fell apart. He lives by himself, and relies on a heavy combination of beer, cigarettes, and unidentified prescription pills to get through the days. By contrast, Chief Brody is still married with young children. Yet both men are driven, particularly after the incidents that disrupt their respective towns, by a fierce desire to protect their communities—especially the children. Both men also gradually become aware of larger forces intent on covering up disturbing information.

Incidentally, the breaking point for each man comes with the concrete realization that a suspected conspiracy theory is actually true. In *Jaws*, the panic surrounding the killer shark is seemingly put to rest when a great white shark is caught. Based on the size of its mouth, however, oceanographer Matt Hooper (played by Richard Dreyfus) doubts it is the same shark they are looking for. While the Mayor doesn't want to hear it, Chief Brody suspects Hooper may be right.

Together, Chief Brody and Matt Hooper sneak into the facility where the shark is being kept and when they cut it open, their suspicions are confirmed. It is not the killer shark, but rather a shark that seems to have migrated up from the gulf stream with nothing inside it but fish, beer cans and a license plate from Louisiana. In *Stranger Things*, likewise, a decoy dead body is used to pacify the town, but Joyce Byers and Chief Brody suspect it may be a deception.

Just as in *Jaws*, Chief Hopper learns the truth by breaking into a facility and cutting open a body—in this case, the decoy corpse of Will. The body is filled with stuffing, definitively confirming a conspiracy to cover up the disappearance of Will. Chief Hopper validates Joyce (who felt as if she was going crazy—and was perceived as such), just as Chief Brody and Matt Hooper validate each other, empowering them to continue their push for the truth.

Another major connection between *Stranger Things* and *Jaws* are the terrifying creatures lurking just beneath (or beyond) the placid surface. One of Spielberg's most brilliant decisions in *Jaws* (necessitated in part by the malfunctioning of the mechanical shark) was to not let the audience see the shark for a good chunk of the movie. It's presence, instead, was suggested—with the primal two-note musical theme, the ominous sight of a fin, or in brief, violent flashes.

Likewise, in *Stranger Things*, we don't see the monster in full for much of the first season. In fact, for most of Season 1 we aren't even quite sure what it is. When we do see it, it is often partially obscured or in quick shots. This was intentional on the part of the Duffer Brothers, who described their monster as "an interdimensional being that has more in common with the shark from *Jaws* than Pennywise from *It*. When the monster enters our dimension, it's like a shark breaching the water. Very much like a shark, it drags its prey back into its home, where it feeds. Each time it enters our world, it leaves a small tear, or wound."

Mark Steger, who plays the monster in *Stranger Things*, acknowledged drawing inspiration from the shark in *Jaws*. "When I come into our consensus reality it's like I'm breaking the surface. [It's like] I'm jumping out and grabbing [*Jaws* actor] Robert Shaw and pulling him back into the deep."

Indeed, the death of Barb (played by Shannon Purser) takes place in a very *Jaws*-like way: she sits on the diving board, her feet dangling into Steve's pool. The eerie calm is disrupted when a drop of blood falls from her finger into the water. The blood seems to attract the monster, who suddenly snatches her sight unseen in the night.

The scene bears a number of resemblances to the shark attacks in *Jaws*: from the attraction to blood, to the proximity to water, to the sudden shock associated with the strike (blood also attracts the demogorgon in the season finale, both at the Byers house, when Nancy and Jonathan intentionally cut their hands, and at Hawkins Middle School, after Eleven kills several agents). The monster, like the shark, is, as Mark Steger puts it, "a perfect eating machine," even more terrifying because of how elusive and shrouded it is in mystery.

Close Encounters

In addition to *Jaws* and *E.T.*, another significant Spielberg touchstone for *Stranger Things* is *Close Encounters of the Third Kind* (1977). Just as Chief Hopper reminded people of Chief Brody, many saw in Joyce Byers echoes of Roy Neary (played by Richard Dreyfuss)—a similarly zealous figure whose determination to find the truth looks more like a descent into madness to those around him (including his family). This connection was consciously made by the Duffer Brothers. "We knew [Winona Ryder] had a very specific energy," said Matt Duffer, "and we thought we would lean into that, and that led us to talking about Richard Dreyfuss' role in *Close Encounters*...the idea of 'Winona Versus The World,' we loved that idea."

In one of the most memorable scenes in *Close Encounters*, a monomaniacal Roy turns his plate of mashed potatoes into a model of Devil's Tower, which he can't get out of his mind. "Everyone thinks he's making a mountain out of mashed potatoes," explains

Matt Duffer. "And I thought: I want to see Winona making a mountain out of mashed potatoes. That's gonna be a great scene."

In Joyce's case the mashed potatoes are the Christmas lights. In Season 1, Chapter 3 ("Holly Jolly"), when she nails the multi-colored lights up all over her house with painted letters on the wall, claiming that it is allowing her to communicate with Will, even her sympathetic son Jonathan thinks she's gone off the deep end. Jonathan's tears as his mother clings to Christmas lights and conspiracy theories echo the dinner table scene in *Close Encounters* when Roy's family is likewise brought to tears by his growing obsession.

Incidentally, Joyce's Christmas lights also recall the climax of *Close Encounters*—the colorful blinking lights transformed into an elaborate system of paranormal communication.

Yet perhaps the most striking connection between *Close Encounters* and *Stranger Things* comes in Season 2, Chapter 1 ("MADMAX"). Near the beginning of the episode, Will finds his surroundings in the arcade suddenly transformed into the Upside Down. He is alone and walks outside, where he looks out at an ominous, gathering storm. This encounter is repeated near the end of the episode: framed by the doorway, he stares out at an apocalyptic red sky. This frame is almost identical to the iconic scene in *Close Encounters* when little Barry Guiler is drawn to the light from a keyhole, and opens the door, mesmerized by the orange light emanating from the encroaching space ships. This visual was also used as cover art for *Stranger Things 2*.

Indiana Jones

A perhaps less immediately obvious Spielberg connection to *Stranger Things* is the *Indiana Jones Trilogy*. Chief Hopper recalls Indiana Jones in a number of ways: the regular-person-by day, adventure-hero-by-night motif; the laconic witticism; the proclivity to land a good punch; even the iconic hat.

Some of the more explicit connections, however, come in Season 2, particularly to *Indiana Jones and the Temple of Doom* (which, not coincidentally, came out in 1984, the year Season 2 takes place). The Duffers acknowledged wanting Season 2 to model the darker tone of *Temple of the Doom*. "I love that it gets a little darker and weirder from *Raiders*," said Matt, "I like that it feels very different than *Raiders* did. Even though it was probably slammed at the time—obviously now people look back on it fondly, but it messed up a lot of kids, and I love that about that film—that it really traumatized some children. Not saying that we want to traumatize children, just that we want to get a little darker and weirder."

One of those darker moments is Will's exorcism. Possessed by the Mind Flayer and wracked with pain, Nancy ultimately decides to grab a hot poker out of the fire and stick it in him in an attempt liberate him from the grip of the monster. This moment is similar to the scene in Temple of Doom when Indiana Jones is possessed until he is brought to his senses by Short Round, who likewise uses fire—in his case, a torch—to save his friend.

Stranger Things also draws on some of *Temple of Doom*'s lighter moments. When Nancy and Jonathan visit Murray Bauman and are trying to figure out the sleeping arrangement in Chapter 6 ("The Spy"), it closely resembles the dynamic between Indy and Willie in Temple of Doom. They want to sleep together, but are reticent to admit it. Explained Matt Duffer of the scene: "that's the whole bedroom dance. Leaving the bedroom, fighting, going back out, coming back, that's *Temple of Doom*."

Another funny moment comes in Chapter 9 ("The Gate"), as Max (played by Sadie Sink) drives the car with a block under her foot to help her reach the gas pedal. "That's exactly like Short Round in *Temple of Doom*," Ross Duffer acknowledges.

The *Indiana Jones* connection is probably most apparent in Chapter 5 ("Dig Dug") as Chief Hopper makes his way through the dark, intricate tunnels underground. The terrain—from the cavernous pathways, to the vines, to the snake-like creatures—all recall the creepy, claustrophobic terrain faced by Indiana Jones. In fact, at one point, Hopper is framed in silhouette with his hat in a visual that could almost be mistaken for Indiana Jones.

Perhaps the best nod of all is when Chief Hopper returns to retrieve his hat—an iconic Indiana Jones move from *Temple of Doom.* Said Ross Duffer of the scene: "Andrew Stanton, who directed [the] episode [added the hat in because] it wasn't in the script, but he's like, 'Hopper's gotta leave his hat and he's gonna grab it.' See, none of us can stop ourselves from doing these references, it's so much fun."

Jurassic Park

While *Jurassic Park* came out in the 1990s—1993 to be exact—its influence on *Stranger Things* is too prominent to ignore. *Jurassic Park* was arguably Spielberg's last major "popcorn movie"—at least until the release of the '80s-inflected 2018 blockbuster *Ready Player One*. Like his biggest movies from the 70s and '80s, *Jurassic Park* was a massive success, grossing over 900 million dollars while saturating popular culture.

The first scene in *Stranger Things* that echoes *Jurassic Park* comes in Season 1, Chapter 1, when Will runs inside his house, trying to escape the Demogorgon. As he picks up the phone to try to get help, we see and hear the monster through the front door window. Its sounds and movements eerily resemble the velociraptors from *Jurassic Park*, specifically, the scene in which the raptors peak in the kitchen door window. Just as in that memorable scene, the demogorgon slowly manages to open the door.

The influence of *Jurassic Park* really begins to emerge, however, in the latter half of Season 2, as the raptor-like demodogs begin to wreak havoc on Hawkins. Compare, for example, the scene in Chapter 6 ("The Spy") when Steve goes out in the junkyard to confront the demodog, before realizing he is surrounded by a pack, to the famous scene in *Jurassic Park* when Robert Muldoon is hunting down a velociraptor only to realize he has fallen into the hyper-intelligent dinosaurs' trap. Like Steve, he is surrounded, leading to his memorable line: "clever girl."

The *Jurassic Park* references come fast and furious in Chapter 8 ("The Mind Flayer") as the demodogs infiltrate Hawkins Lab. When Jonathan and Nancy meet up with Steve and the kids just outside the building, the shrieks they hear in the distance sound a lot like the dinosaurs in *Jurassic Park*. Meanwhile, inside the facility, as in *Jurassic Park*, the power must be restored, but reaching the breakers proves daunting. In *Jurassic Park*, Dr. Sattler accepts the mission as park creator John Hammond gives instructions via walkie talkie. In *Stranger Things*, the task is carried out by Bob Newby as Dr. Owens delivers directions, also by walkie talkie.

As Bob makes his way through the dark corridors and stairwells of the Lab, the visuals feel very similar to *Jurassic Park*, as does the urgency of the mission and the tension of surrounding threats. Like Dr. Sattler, Bob is able to successfully reach the breakers and restore power. Yet like Dr. Sattler, the return proves more difficult. Bob's retreat into a storage closet is a very *Jurassic Park*-like moment—the demodogs, like the dinosaurs, are sensitive to sound and movement. Bob is able to stay quiet and still until the monster has passed, but as he attempts to escape he accidentally tips over a broom.

Dr. Owens shouting, "Run!" echoes Dr. Sattler shouting the same in Spielberg's film. Bob slamming the door just before the monster reaches him also echoes *Jurassic Park*. While Dr. Sattler narrowly escapes the velociraptors, well….we know what happens to Bob. May he rest in peace.

Poltergeist

There are a number of other Spielberg connections in *Stranger Things*—including to '80s films Spielberg wrote or produced, rather than directed. One direct reference comes in Season 1, Chapter 1 ("The Vanishing of Will Byers") when, in a flashback, Joyce surprises Will with tickets to see the horror movie *Poltergeist*. Released in the summer of 1982, *Poltergeist* was written and produced by Spielberg (a clause in his contract prevented him from directing it). It ended up being directed by Tobe Hooper, best known previously for *The Texas Chainsaw Massacre*, and became one of the biggest movies of that year, grossing over $75 million dollars.

Stranger Things draws from *Poltergeist* in a number of ways. The Duffer Brothers acknowledged thinking a lot about the film when drafting early scripts of the series, particularly the dynamic of an ordinary family losing a child to another dimension. Like the young girl Carol Anne from *Poltergeist*, Will is sucked into an alternate dimension—in his case, the Upside Down. As in *Poltergeist*, much of the ensuing story is driven by a family, with the help of others, trying to rescue a lost child.

Will and Carol Anne also both act as prophetic figures. "They're here," Carol Anne famously warns of the demonic ghosts about to invade her suburban house and town. Similarly, in Season 2, Chapter 1, Will tells Dr. Owen that the Mind Flayer is angry and intends to kill everyone (except him).

Beyond the thematic parallels, there is also a rather striking visual similarity in a shot toward the end of Season 2, Chapter 2 ("Trick or Treat, Freak") when Eleven is watching TV in Chief Hopper's cabin. Shot from behind her head, it very closely resembles the most iconic shot from *Poltergeist* (featured on the cover) of Carol Anne staring at a statticky TV.

Gremlins

The Duffers attributed the influence of an entire episode—Season 2, Chapter 3 ("The Pollywog")—to another classic '80s film Spielberg executive produced: *Gremlins*. That 1984 comedy-horror film about a cute, seemingly harmless creature named Gizmo adopted by a young boy (Billy), which subsequently evolves into something far more dangerous and menacing is the blueprint for Dustin and the pollywog-like creature he names D'Artagnan (Dart for short). In fact, both creatures not only grow; they multiply. Yet in both cases, the original creatures—Gizmo and Dart, respectively—retain a certain loyalty to their masters, while the creatures they have spawned become, in essence, killing machines.

The Gremlins concept was something the Duffers thought of early in planning sessions for Season 2. "Aside from Will being possessed," they told *Vulture*, "that storyline was always baked into our first idea: a boy and his monster, Dustin finding a creature that will grow. That was our first idea for season two."

The Goonies

And then there is *The Goonies*. Like *Poltergeist* and *Gremlins*, Spielberg didn't officially direct *The Goonies* (it was directed by Richard Donner), but his fingerprints are all over it. Not only did he come up with the story and executive produce the movie, he was also on set for much of the movie's production, acting as a kind of uncredited co-director. The movie was a big hit in 1985, and has since become a cult classic.

The Goonies is among the biggest influences on Stranger Things, from the rag-tag assembly of kids and older teenagers, to the presence of bikes, to the labyrinthine network of underground tunnels they navigate, to the curiosity-driven quest. While Stranger Things is definitely more grounded in the horror genre, both share similar tones, balancing adventure, fear, humor, and wonder.

Even some of the more specific character casting decisions in Stranger Things were based on The Goonies. The Duffer Brothers said that Mike Wheeler's character was originally based on Mikey from the 1985 movie—"that Sean Astin soft-spoken dreamer type." That character was tweaked a bit when Finn Wolfhard came on board, but he still retained certain qualities that resemble Mikey, including his focus, sensitivity, and determination.

Incidentally, the actor that played Mikey in The Goonies—Sean Astin—joined Stranger Things in Season 2 as Bob Newby, who became one of the show's most beloved characters. While his character is obviously very different than in The Goonies, the Duffers managed to work in a clever nod to the movie when Bob is helping the boys make sense of Will's interconnected drawings. Mike explains to Bob that they are trying to find the X within Will's intricate maze. "What's at the X?" Bob jokes. "Pirate treasure?"

Pirate treasure, of course, is exactly what Mikey and his pals were led to in The Goonies by the map of the infamous pirate, One-eyed Willie. "Sean loved [the reference]," said Matt Duffer, "he was totally game for it. He loves to talk about [The Goonies], thankfully. We asked him about it all day, and the kids are big fans so they'd pester him about it all day."

Other characters in Stranger Things were also clearly inspired by The Goonies: Dustin plays a more compelling variation of Chunk—a rambunctious, funny, food-loving kid who features in some of the show's best moments of comic relief. Jonathan (played by Charlie Heaton) echoes Brand (played by Josh Brolin)—quiet, brooding guys who don't quite fit into the scene at school, but possess a certain coolness that intrigues the girls.

In *The Goonies*, Brand manages to win the affection of the pretty, popular Andy, while Jonathan eventually hooks up with Nancy (although it should be noted that Steve wears the Brand-like red bandana when they descend into the tunnels in Season 2).

Perhaps the most widely-noted character parallel is between Stef and Barb, both of whom play quirky, nerdy, loyal sidekicks to the popular girl (Andy and Nancy, respectively). The similarities don't stop there. Both are put in the uncomfortable position of "third wheel." Both have red hair. And both have a similar sense of style (see the large-framed glasses and mom jeans).

More broadly, *Stranger Things* models the dynamic in *The Goonies* of having intermingled storylines for both the high school generation as well as for the younger group of kids, thereby appealing to both generations of viewers.

A New Voice

Every movie mentioned in this chapter was made between 1975-1993. It represents a remarkable explosion of influential output from Spielberg. In fact, five of the eight movies mentioned were made between 1982 and 1985, the exact period in which *Stranger Things* takes place. And three movies—*Jaws*, *E.T.*, and *Jurassic Park*—at one time held the title of highest-grossing film of all time.

It is no wonder, then, that *Stranger Things* references Spielberg so much: his early movies not only transformed cinema; they were part of the zeitgeist. According to producer Shawn Levy, the references to Spielberg's movies are less "deliberate" homages than an instinctive, subconscious influence—as he put it, his films run "through our veins."

While Spielberg hasn't spoken publicly about *Stranger Things*, Levy says the director has reached out behind the scenes and been "so complimentary." When he and the Duffers speak to Spielberg, says Levy, "We don't talk about the fact that it's got nods to him left and right, but I think that's the unspoken, acknowledged flattery inherent in the show. He, frankly, like me, sees in the brothers the arrival of a new voice."

That new voice certainly owes a great deal to Spielberg; but there are a number of other cinematic influences the show draws on as well. Not surprisingly, most were made in the '80s. Those inspirations are explored in the next chapter.

3

'80s Movies

When the Duffer Brothers pitched *Stranger Things*, they presented a mashup of around thirty movies—most of them from the '80s—that conveyed their vision for the series. It was an eclectic motley of genres, styles, and directors. As pervasive as Spielberg's influence was on the show, it was fusing that aesthetic with a wide range of other influences that made the series truly compelling and unique. "John Carpenter mashed up with *E.T.* was really cool," said Matt Duffer. "So that was where we started to figure out the tone of the show."

The John Carpenter reference is an important one. Along with Spielberg and Stephen King, John Carpenter is perhaps the third-most cited name in the Duffer Brothers' Holy Trinity of influences. Yet unlike the former two figures, Carpenter is not a household name—his films have developed a cult following, but they were nowhere near the blockbuster phenomena of Spielberg and King.

Still, John Carpenter is highly regarded among film buffs, particularly fans of horror movies, the genre in which he made his biggest mark. His most influential film, *Halloween*, was a low-budget movie about a boy—Michael Myers—who kills his sister, gets sent to an asylum, and returns years later to wreak havoc on his hometown in Illinois. Released in 1978, it gained traction by word-of-mouth and ultimately became one of the most popular horror movies of its time, grossing an estimated $70 million dollars on a $300 thousand dollar budget. Some film critics cite it as the father of the modern slasher film and the beginning of a horror renaissance in the 1980s.

It is also known for its moody, minimalist score, which was composed by the director himself. Carpenter would go on to score nearly all of his other movies. "I'm not an accomplished composer of symphonies," the director acknowledged. "I just do basic, straight-ahead, riff-driven music." His limitations, however, gave his music a kind of primal impact. In contrast to the wonder and warmth of *E.T.* is something closer to the chilling terror of *Psycho* or *Jaws*, but with a more contemporary synth-based touch.

We hear strains of that Carpenter pulse, tension, and dread in Kyle Dixon and Michael Stein's music for *Stranger Things*. "We wanted an all-electronic soundtrack," explained Matt Duffer. "In part, just because, I think when you see a story like this that has any sort of Amblin DNA in it, you're going to expect a sort of John Williams orchestral score. We kind of wanted to play against those expectations. We also wanted it to have a slightly darker, John Carpenter edge, so it allowed us to do that."

We also see elements of Carpenter's camera work. *Halloween* begins with a long tracking shot from the point of view of the killer (Michael Myers). Carpenter used a Steadicam for the scene, one of the first directors to really figure out how to use it effectively. We see the house from outside, as the young killer moves from window to window, then to the back door, then up the stairs, and into the dimly lit bedroom. The effect was realistic and heart-pounding.

Similarly, in *Stranger Things*, the Duffers often make use of character-driven camera movement. "We shot on a digital camera," they explained, "but we added film grain, and we wanted to have a very sort of filmic look. We tried to move the camera as much as we could, as long as it was motivated." We also see some of Carpenter's trademark widescreen framing in *Stranger Things*. As director of photography Tim Ives explained: "[Our] approach to lensing was to be a little more cinematic than most shows on television. We went 2:1 on the aspect ratio, so it has this slightly letterboxed feel to it. We really wanted it to feel not like a regular television show—you were meant to be watching something that was an event."

Given Carpenter's influence on the Duffers, it is not surprising that we also see a number of direct references to Carpenter's work in *Stranger Things*. In Season 1, Chapter 2 ("The Weirdo on Maple Street"), as the boys are trying to figure out where Eleven came from, Lucas concludes that "she's probably a psycho." "Like Michael Myers," Dustin chimes in, referencing the infamous villain from *Halloween*. "Exactly!" Lucas responds. In Season 2, Chapter 2 ("Trick or Treat, Freak"), *Halloween* is referenced again as Max wears the iconic white mask dawned by Michael Myers while trick-or-treating.

Other fans have noted similarities to Carpenter's 1980 film, *The Fog*, about a mysterious, supernatural presence that infiltrates a small town. But perhaps the biggest Carpenter influence on *Stranger Things* is *The Thing*. Released in 1982, *The Thing* fell flat at the box office, some believe, because it was competing with *E.T.* In contrast to Spielberg's film, it was bleak and grim. It takes place in Antarctica where a group of American researchers are besieged by a parasitic alien lifeform that takes the shape of whatever it kills. While the movie was lambasted by the public and critics alike in 1982, it has since become a cult classic and garnered recognition as perhaps Carpenter's best film.

Allusions to the film in *Stranger Things* abound. Most obvious is the poster hanging in the Wheeler's basement. Not only does it allow the Duffers to pay tribute to the film, it also suggests that Mike Wheeler and his friends are not only into the big blockbuster franchises. They can also appreciate a deep cut, bleak movie that was out of the mainstream. It also indicates—like Will's interest in *Poltergeist*, that these kids are drawn to some pretty scary movies—in the case of *The Thing*, a movie so gory and violent it received an R-rating (for context, *Jaws* was rated PG).

The Thing is also referenced in Season 1, Chapter 7 ("The Bathtub"), when Dustin makes a late-night call to Mr. Clarke, to inquire about how to build a sensory-deprivation tank. Mr. Clarke is on a date, watching a VHS home video of *The Thing*. They are at the part where a possessed Norris (played by Charlie Hallahan) is torched, his decapitated head slowly falling to the ground. "You know how they did that?" Mr. Clarke tells his date. "You know what that is? Melted plastic and microwaved bubblegum."

More broadly, *Stranger Things* draws on *The Thing's* premise of an alien life form invading, possessing and controlling the human body—which, in the case of *Stranger Things*, happens to Will. Note also the worm-like tentacles that reach down Will's throat, which vividly recall the alien's method of invasion in *The Thing*. Indeed, one of the ways *Stranger Things* seems most inspired by *The Thing* is through the film's slimy, tactile, gruesome special effects. In Carpenter's film, those groundbreaking effects were created by Rob Bottin, with assistance from the legendary Stan Winston.

It is more common now for such effects to appear CGI-pristine and smooth, but *Stranger Things* gives its creatures—and the Upside Down—a very textured, tangible feel that recalls '80s horror films like *The Thing*. "Like so many filmmakers our age and older," the Duffer Brothers explained, "we grew up on genre films that existed before computer graphics. There was something about the effects being so tangible in those films that made them especially terrifying to us when we were kids."

Accordingly, the Duffer Brothers brought in a company called Spectral Motion to create a very organic-feeling monster using a real person (Mark Steger) in a prosthetic body suit with animatronic movements. Some CGI effects were also added. But the end result felt very reminiscent of '80s movies like *The Thing*. Wrote the Duffer Brothers: "The first time we saw our monster's head peel open…it just blew our minds and transported us back to our childhood. And the *way* it moved was terrifying—their brilliant robotics engineer had designed the animatronics in such a way that the movement of the head "petals" never repeated themselves. They had a life of their own, moving in unpredictable and bizarre patterns. It felt organic. Creepy. *Real*."

The Horror

John Carpenter's films ignited a renaissance in the horror genre—especially the slasher film—which became hugely popular in the 1980s, led by the *Friday the 13th* and *Nightmare on Elm Street* franchises. We see echoes of these films in *Stranger Things*, both of which similarly feature teenagers battling dangerous, predatory figures. In *Nightmare on Elm Street*, that figure is Freddy Krueger, who stalks and attacks the characters in their dreams (which, like Will's visions, become increasingly indistinguishable from reality). The scene in Season 1, Chapter 2 ("The Weirdo on Maple Street"), when Steve and Nancy are getting intimate in his bedroom, while Barb is attacked by the demogorgon carries traces of *Nightmare on Elm Street*, as does the scene when Nancy and Jonathan set traps for the monster throughout the Byers' house, eventually lighting him on fire, in Chapter 8 ("The Upside Down").

The Duffer Brothers have cited a number of lesser-known horror films that inspired them, including the low-budget 1981 indie film *The Evil Dead* (a poster of the movie hangs in Jonathan's bedroom). *Stranger Things* also draws on a relatively unknown 1980 sci-fi-horror cult classic, *Altered States*, about a psychologist (Edward Jessup) who conducts experiments with sensory deprivation tanks and psychoactive drugs in an attempt to access expanded states of consciousness. Incidentally, the film also marked the debut role of Drew Barrymore, who most people were introduced to a couple of years later as Gertie in *E.T.*

The Breakfast Club

As important as John Carpenter and '80s horror films are to *Stranger Things*, however, it is by no means the only significant cinematic influence. A large part of the show's appeal has as much to do with its depiction of the social experience of high school (and middle school)—the relationships, the cliques, styles, tensions, and drama—as the extraterrestrial monsters and gruesome standoffs. In fact, one could argue that *Stranger Things* is as at least as much indebted to John Hughes as it is to John Carpenter.

Who is John Hughes? For those who didn't grow up in the '80s, he was the man who, in essence, created the blueprint for Gen-X high school movies, helping inspire what many film critics now describe as the golden era of movies about teenagers. His films took adolescents seriously: their relationships, their music, their internal conflicts, their desires. They were also very funny. His catalog of '80s classics includes *Sixteen Candles* (1984), *Weird Science* (1985), *The Breakfast Club* (1985), *Ferris Bueller's Day Off* (1986), and *Pretty in Pink* (1986). He also helped launch the careers of a generation of young actors, including Molly Ringwald, Jon Cryer, Emilio Estevez, and Matthew Broderick.

Many of these films, like *Stranger Things*, are set in the midwest (often in suburban Illinois). They also feature similar musical tastes. In *Pretty in Pink*, for example, we hear several bands also featured in *Stranger Things*: Psychedelic Furs, The Smiths, Echo and the Bunnymen, and New Order (these songs are explored in greater depth in Chapter 4 of this book). In fact, New Order's "Elegia" is featured prominently in both *Pretty in Pink* and *Stranger Things* (in Season 1, Chapter 4). They also share a love affair with David Bowie. *The Breakfast Club* famously opens with a quote from the alternative pop icon:

> *...And these children*
> *that you spit on*
> *as they try to change their worlds*
> *are immune to your consultations.*
> *They're quite aware of what they're going through...*

Bowie plays a similar role in *Stranger Things*—his poster is on Jonathan's wall, and his song "Heroes," is featured in Season 1, Chapter 4 ("The Body"). In Season 2, Chapter 1 ("MADMAX") Jonathan uses him as a model for why it's okay to be a "freak."

Beyond the music, many of the types and social dynamics in *Stranger Things* are very much from the playbook of John Hughes films: the sexual angst and love triangles, the class tensions, the cool kids (Steve) and eccentric outsiders (Jonathan), nerdy sidekicks (Barb) and class clowns (Dustin), tomboys (Max) and bad boys (Billy).

The dynamic between Steve, Nancy and Jonathan is particularly John Hughes-esque. The trope of the more studious girl attracting the more popular boy is all over '80s teen movies. Yet the hallmark of a John Hughes movie is allowing the outsiders to somehow prevail. This is exactly what happens in *Stranger Things* as

Nancy gradually loses interest in Steve and begins to fall in love with the more intriguing and eccentric Jonathan.

While Steve loses out on Nancy, his character reveals another common trope in Hughes movies: the redemption of the douche (this is discussed in greater depth in Chapter 10 of this book). Steve, who we first get to know as the handsome, but rich, entitled boyfriend, gradually matures into a more sensitive, funny, and honorable guy — a transformation that resembles the character evolution of Andrew Clark (Emilio Estevez) in *The Breakfast Club* or even Blane (Andrew McCarthy) in *Pretty in Pink*.

The brother-sister dynamic between Nancy and Mike, meanwhile, has traces of Ferris (Matthew Broderick) and Jeanie (Jennifer Grey) from *Ferris Bueller's Day Off*. Like Ferris, Mike fakes sick to stay home, and his parents remain oblivious to his real activities. Incidentally, Joe Keery (who plays Steve Harrington) also riffed on *Ferris Bueller's Day Off* in a popular 2017 commercial for Domino's pizza.

Hughes wasn't the only director capturing the teenage experience on film in the '80s. Among other big teen movies were: *Fast Times at Ridgemont High* (1982), *Risky Business* (1983), *All the Right Moves* (1983), *The Outsiders* (1983), *Footloose* (1984), *St. Elmo's Fire* (1985), *Back to the Future* (1985), *Dirty Dancing* (1987), *Can't Buy Me Love* (1987), and *Say Anything* (1989).

There are references in *Stranger Things* to some of these films as well. Billy's look is modelled in many ways after Rob Lowe's character from *St. Elmo's Fire* (also named Billy). In Season 1, Chapter 5 ("The Flea and the Monster"), Steve invites Nancy on a date to see *All the Right Moves*, starring Tom Cruise (who is also featured on a poster on Nancy's bedroom wall). When Nancy hedges, Steve launches into a rendition of "Old Time Rock n' Roll," like Cruise's character Joel in *Risky Business*. In Season 2, Chapter 2 ("Trick or

Treat, Freak") Nancy and Steve also dress up as the characters — Joel and Lana — from *Risky Business* for the Halloween party.

Perhaps the greatest '80s teen movie moment in *Stranger Things* comes in the finale of Season 2 at the Hawkins Middle School Snow Ball Dance. Here, we have all the key ingredients of the genre on full display: the awkwardness and anticipation, the crosscurrents of interest (or lack thereof), the music, the hair.

Eleven's physical transformation is a classic '80s trope, recalling Andy from *Pretty in Pink* as well as Allison from *The Breakfast Club*. But Dustin's experience is perhaps most evocative. After a pep talk from Steve, he walks into the dance anxious, but resolved to go for it. Yet as the slow-dancing begins, his prospects begin to dwindle: Lucas gets Max (Dustin's first choice); then he is rudely rejected by the popular girl, Stacy. As he looks around for a partner, girls look away. Eventually, he ends up alone on the bleachers, in tears. Many viewers made connections between Dustin and Duckie, the eccentric and nerdy, but loveable character from *Pretty in Pink*.

Like Duckie, Dustin doesn't ultimately get the girl he wants. But he does get to dance with Nancy, who sees him sitting by himself, and compassionately builds him back up as the popular girls look on in amazement. It is a very '80s-teen-movie moment, further amplified by the goosebump-inducing reunion of Mike and Eleven. Looming over the building, of course, is a sinister, supernatural presence certainly not found in any John Hughes movie: the Mind Flayer. That brings us back to the realm of science fiction.

Aliens

Perhaps the biggest sci-fi influence on *Stranger Things* — beyond Spielberg's films — is the *Alien* franchise. Released in 1979, the first *Alien* movie was directed by Ridley Scott, and became a massive hit, grossing over $79 million in its first run. It told the story of a space crew, awakened from their sleep pods by a distress call, who subsequently face off against a vicious, parasitic alien that hatches inside their spaceship. The film's screenwriters famously pitched it as "Jaws in space." In this way, it was one of the first major films to combine the genres of horror and science fiction.

The Duffer have acknowledged the influence of *Alien* on *Stranger Things*, particularly in its *Jaws*-like slow-build dread and restraint. "We looked a lot at Ridley Scott's *Alien*," says Ross Duffer. "On YouTube, there's a cut of all the instances where you see the alien in that first movie, and it's a couple minutes long. And that's a two-hour movie. I think the reason it's so scary is that, when it does appear, it has a certain amount of impact. So we thought, OK, we're going to see the shadow in Episode 1, because we knew we had eight episodes. We were trying to slowly reveal it, until you finally saw the full thing."

We see a number of visual resemblances to *Alien* in *Stranger Things*, most clearly when Chief Hopper and Joyce enter the portal into the Upside Down in Season 1, Chapter 8 "(The Upside Down")," in hazmat suits with flashlights. The slimy textures and dark, damp, claustrophobic atmosphere, the cobweb-like cocoons, the mouth-penetrating tentacles all recall *Alien*. Moreover, while their faces are obviously different, some of the the Demogorgon's movements, methods of attack, and overall feel seem to draw from the alien in Ridley Scott's film. In addition, the shrieking sound it makes when being killed and the gooey residue it leaves behind are very similar.

Just as influential (if not more) on *Stranger Things* is the 1986 sequel, *Aliens*, directed by James Cameron. A great deal of buzz accompanied this sequel, as fans of the original movie waited seven years for it. Many, however, doubted it would be as good as the first, given the trend of declining returns with other franchises (see *Jaws*). Yet *Aliens* was even more successful at the box office than the original, generating over $85 million and becoming one of the most lucrative R-rated films to that point. It was also widely praised by critics for staying true to the aesthetic of the original, while adding more brisk-paced action.

As the Duffer Brothers began brainstorming for Season 2 of *Stranger Things*, they often used *Aliens* as a reference point. "We talked about *Aliens* because we were looking at the most successful sequels of all time, and *Aliens* is arguably one of the most successful sequels," explained Matt Duffer. "I love that people argue over whether *Alien* or *Aliens* is better, and I've changed my mind a hundred times. It takes a lot of the feelings and a lot of what worked about *Alien*, and then James Cameron did this amazing pivot almost into another genre. He expanded the scope and made it feel the same but also very different. When you're looking at where the bar is, I always go to *Aliens*. Naturally, we wanted to give a couple of nods to it."

Those nods began early in the first season of the series, and continue more prominently in Season 2. For example, in the opening scene of Season 1, Chapter 1 ("The Vanishing of Will Byers"), when the man in a lab coat frantically rushes down a flickering hallway to the elevator, before being snatched from above by a demogorgon, it is reminiscent of a number of elevator scenes in *Aliens*, including one in which Ripley (played by Sigourney Weaver) rushes a young girl (Newt) to an elevator, frantically pushing the buttons, as they try to escape the Alien queen.

There is also the introduction of Dr. Owens, played by Paul Reiser, who also featured in *Aliens* as Carter Burke. Producer Shawn Levy, in fact, revealed that in the original Season 2 screenplay Dr. Owens was actually called Dr. Reiser. In *Aliens*, Reiser plays a smarmy corporate representative sent to investigate LV-426 who, over the course of the film, we learn is more invested in the interests of the company than helping the crew. He ultimately becomes the film's primary human antagonist.

In certain ways, that role is reprised with Dr. Owens, who runs the show at Hawkins National Laboratory in the wake of Dr. Brenner's absence. Paul Reiser described his new character as "a spiritual nephew" to his role as Burke in *Aliens*. While his personality seems earnest and amiable enough, the audience is skeptical of him from the outset—perhaps in part because of the Burke association, but also simply because he works for the Laboratory. Yet over the course of Season 2, his character charts a different trajectory than his character in *Aliens*. Yes, he admits to keeping the truth about many of the Hawkins Lab's nefarious activities from the public. But there are reasons. For proof, he begins to show Hopper, as well as Nancy and Jonathan, behind the curtain at Hawkins Lab.

While Dr. Owens, like Burke in Aliens, is an establishment figure, around the midpoint of Season 2 the Duffer Brothers slowly and subtly begin to reveal new wrinkles to his character. Turns out, he may not be a bad guy after all. As television critic Abraham Reissman explains: "While everyone else runs in search of safety, he sticks around to help Bob the Brain get out alive." In that effort, he is ultimately unsuccessful—and suffers near-fatal injuries himself. But unlike in *Aliens*, in which he deceives and betrays his fellow crew members—finally abandoning them to preserve his own life—in *Stranger Things* he does the opposite. In fact, we even learn that he was the only one at Hawkins Lab who stood up for Will and found a way to get Hopper custody of Eleven. In this way, as Reisman puts it, "*Stranger Things* is doing what it does best: not just mimicking the art of the 1980s, but twisting it into something new and delightful."

There are a number of other parallels to *Aliens*: Eleven's short, curly hair style in Season 2 is very similar to Ripley's in *Aliens*; Joyce's passionate rants against the bureaucrats at Hawkins Lab recall Ripley's tirade against the Weyland-Yutani Company; the demogorgon multiplying into pollywogs and demodogs is reminiscent of the alien reproducing and multiplying in *Aliens*; the shrieking cats sensing something dangerous; the plant-like petals of the eggs hatching in *Aliens* looks very similar to the face of the demogorgon in *Stranger Things*; the Hawkins lab agents spraying fire is similar to the torch guns used in *Aliens*.

Season 2, Chapter 6 ("The Spy") is particularly indebted to *Aliens*. "Andrew Stanton directed that episode, had storyboards up and they were shot for shot storyboards from Aliens," revealed David Harbour. "Same scene, Paul Reiser in the same position." In fact, there is even a direct line from Cameron's film. As the soldiers descend into the underground tunnels, Dr. Owens and others look on through grainy monitors, recalling the scene in *Aliens* when Ripley, Burke and company do the same as the soldiers scour the exo-moon LV-426. Just like in *Aliens*, one of the soldiers says, "Stay frosty, boys!" And just as in *Aliens*, the expedition doesn't end well.

Incidentally, Season 2 also makes a couple of references to another James Cameron blockbuster: *The Terminator*, which was released in 1984, the year the second season takes place. We first see it on the theater marquee in downtown Hawkins. In Chapter 2 ("Trick or Treat, Freak"), it pops up again, this time as a movie preview as Eleven flips through channels on the TV.

Star Wars

Another major sci-fi influence on *Stranger Things* is the original *Star Wars* trilogy. Like Spielberg's movies, every kid growing up in the '80s knew *Star Wars*. Its characters, quotes, and mythology were part of the air we breathed. Moreover, while *A New Hope* was released in 1977, *Empire Strikes Back* (1980) and *Return of the Jedi* (1983) were released in the '80s, so it was still very fresh on the scene when *Stranger Things* takes place. The sequels were massive successes, each grossing over $200 million domestically and $400 million worldwide. Its saturation in popular culture was simply unparalleled, from toys to costumes to games.

We see that saturation in *Stranger Things*. In Mike's house, for example, we see a toy Millenium Falcon, as well as a Yoda figurine. It wasn't easy getting these toys on the show, the Duffers revealed, due to licensing issues. "It's funny," admitted Matt Duffer, "if you'll notice in Episode 3, the [Millenium] Falcon is actually hidden under a blanket because you can't be showing it in every scene. We were really excited that we got to put in some "Star Wars" toys...Lucasfilm was super cool to let us do that."

Those toys are more than just props in *Stranger Things*. When Mike is showing Eleven around his room in Season 1, Chapter 2 ("The Weirdo on Maple Street"), he imitates Yoda, before explaining that the Jedi Master "can use the Force to move things with his mind." Eleven, of course, does just that with another Star Wars toy, the Millenium Falcon in Chapter 3 ("Holly, Jolly"). In subsequent episodes her powers are often compared by the boys to the powers of a Jedi. The way she focuses her mind and sometimes uses her hands even looks similar to the way the Force is deployed in *Star Wars*.

In addition to comparing Eleven to a Jedi, the kids make a number of other references to *Star Wars*. In Season 1, Chapter 6 ("The Monster"), for example, Dustin compares confronting the Demogorgon with a wrist rocket (and without Eleven) to R2D2 going against Darth Vader. In Season 1, Chapter 7 ("The Bathtub"), a number of allusions are made to Lando Calrissian, the character who betrays Han Solo in *Empire Strikes Back*. Lucas refers to Eleven as Lando after believing she lied to them about the whereabouts of Will. Later on in the bus, Dustin makes the reference several times when trying to determine whether Nancy and Chief Hopper's pleas on the walkie talkie are "a trap." In Season 2, Chapter 3 ("The Pollywog"),

Mike counters Dustin's argument that just because his pollywog might be from the Upside Down doesn't mean it's bad, retorting: "That's like saying, just because someone's from the Death Star, doesn't make him bad."

There are character parallels as well. Eleven's journey and evolution is similar to that of Luke Skywalker, particularly in how she discovers and uses her power. This is apparent throughout Seasons 1 and 2, as El uses her ability to help and save people as well as to hurt people. The Duffers acknowledged that *Star Wars* was particularly relevant as they thought through Season 2, Chapter 7 ("The Lost Sister"). "Just like Luke Skywalker, [El] needed to go off on her own and learn something about herself," explained Ross Duffer.

In particular, they "talked a lot about *Empire Strikes Back*," says Matt Duffer. "…about Luke going to Dagobah and meeting Yoda. Also, the idea of a dark Eleven, of Eleven being pulled to the dark side was an interesting idea. So a lot of that episode was what happens if Eleven is drawn towards this darkness and what can she learn about herself if that's the case."

We see the *Star Wars* dynamic at play throughout Chapter 7. Compare, for example, Eleven moving the freight train with her mind to Luke moving the spaceship from the Dagobah swamp in *Empire Strikes Back*. Their mentors, of course, are different. In place of Yoda is El's long-lost sister, Kali, who in some ways represents a kind of shadow figure for El, just as Darth Vader does for Luke.

Linnea Berthelsen, who played Kali, acknowledged thinking about this dynamic in preparing for her character. "I took everything from Luke and from the relationship with Anakin," she says. "The reason why Kali is so angry is also because of love. She wants to believe in another human being. Something really went wrong and people let her down. She's trying what she believes is the best way to support Eleven. Maybe it's not the right way to do it but it's coming from a good place. And I think that's the same thing with Darth Vader — he believes it's the right thing and he's doing everything for the love of his mother."

There is also a Luke-Darth Vader dynamic with Eleven and Papa. El seems to sense some good in him, even though he appears to be a very dark, sinister figure. We get the sense, just as in *Star Wars*, that more will be revealed on that front in coming seasons.

Star Wars, then, is a crucial touchstone in *Stranger Things* — both as a mythological well from which to draw themes and ideas, as well as a cultural presence that seeps into conversations, storylines, and bedrooms.

Ghostbusters

And then there's *Ghostbusters*. Cue the music.

Once the Duffer Brothers decided to set Season 2 in the fall of 1984, they knew they had to have the boys dress up in *Ghostbuster* attire for Halloween. *Ghostbusters* hit theaters in the summer of '84 and became a huge hit, grossing over $240 million dollars in the U.S. It was the bestselling comedy of the decade.

As with *Star Wars*, it took some wrangling to get permission to use the *Ghostbusters* suits and song in *Stranger Things*. The Duffers ultimately made their pitch to the director of the movie himself: Ivan Reitman. "We had this very nervous speech about what *Ghostbusters* meant to us," recalls Matt Duffer. "That movie was a big part of my childhood. We watched that VHS tape *so* many times. I had it memorized. Anyway, it was very easy for me to talk passionately about *Ghostbusters,* and he made us go through the exercise, but he'd already decided to let us do it. He was like, 'We're very flattered by it. Of course we'd love to have you use it.' And we were like, 'Phew!'"

Ghostbusters is on full display in Season 2, Chapter 2 ("Trick or Treat, Freak"), as the kids strike poses for Polaroid pictures. When they meet up at school, they debate the relative coolness of characters from the movie, after Mike and Lucas discover they both chose Venkman (played by Bill Murray). No one wants to be Winston (played by Ernie Hudson), because, as Lucas puts it: "He joined the team super late, he's not funny, and he's not even a scientist."

Some saw the incorporation of *Ghostbusters* as gimmicky, but the Duffers defended the decision on the grounds that they and their friends actually dressed up as Ghostbusters. "These kids would be into *Ghostbusters*," argued Matt Duffer. "To me, that's authentic. That's not self-aware. It's authentic, it's real, because we did it."

As we will see in the next chapter, the same calculation was made for music. In fact, the appearance of Ray Parker Jr.'s hit song, "Ghostbusters," makes perfect sense for Season 2. The song was a massive hit in 1984 and would have been all over the radio that summer and fall, especially leading up to Halloween. That authenticity—both to the era and to the story and characters—is the modus operandi for most of the music featured in the series.

4

'80s Music

No single song is as important to *Stranger Things* as The Clash's 1982 classic, "Should I Stay or Should I Go."

We first hear the track in Season 1, Chapter 2 ("The Weirdo on Maple Street"), as Jonathan is driving his car. The song triggers a flashback to several months before Will's disappearance. The brothers are hanging out in his bedroom, listening to a mixtape Jonathan made for Will, including songs by The Clash, Joy Division, Television, The Smiths, and David Bowie. "It will totally change your life," he tells Will.

In the background, we hear their parents fighting, which, it is suggested by Will's reaction, is a common occurrence. To drown out the yelling, Jonathan turns up the music. The song, in this way, not only bonds the brothers; it provides a kind of emotional shield against the pain and disappointments they face together, including the divorce of their parents.

"Should I Stay or Should I Go" is among The Clash's most famous songs. Part rockabilly, part punk, with a killer guitar riff, it peaked at just #45 on the Billboard Hot 100, but was universally known in the alternative scene and has since become regarded as one of the best songs of the decade. *Rolling Stone* included the track on their "500 Greatest Songs of All Time" list (ranking #228).

It seems probable that Jonathan would have bought the entire album—*Combat Rock*—which was released in June 1982, and also featured the hit song, "Rock the Casbah." Much of that album critiqued America's foreign policy and moral decay. This was no surprise to followers of the band. In the late '70s and early '80s, being a fan of The Clash was not just about the music; it was a declaration of identity. The Clash represented rebellion, dissent, and resistance to mainstream values.

Particularly after the release of *London Calling* in 1980, which some music critics praised as the best album of the decade, they were widely regarded as the greatest punk band of their generation. They were often referred to as "The Only Band That Matters," a promotional slogan that became a kind of cultural truism to their underground following.

It's easy, then, to see their appeal to Jonathan. The cover of "Should I Stay or Should I Go" featured a grainy picture of Ronald Reagan, suggesting the question in the title might have political implications. Yet at the time, many actually interpreted it in more personal terms—as lead singer Mick Jones contemplating whether or not to leave the band (as it turned out, the *Combat Rock* was The Clash's last album with the original lineup).

But what is its significance to *Stranger Things*? Besides capturing the sound and feel of the early '80s and giving a sense of Jonathan's musical tastes, it also plays a significant role in the story, serving as a means of connection and foreshadowing the difficult conundrum facing Will.

"Should I Stay or Should I Go" resurfaces multiple times throughout Seasons 1 and 2. In Chapter 2 ("The Weirdo on Maple Street"), Will uses it to communicate with his mother Joyce from the

Upside Down, making the song play on the boombox in his bedroom (note how, at that moment, Joyce must decide whether to stay at the house or go). We hear the song again in Chapter 4 ("The Body"), as Eleven manages to channel Will's faint voice singing through the walkie talkie. Will is also humming the song as he hides in Castle Byers, shivering as the Monster nears in Chapter 7 ("The Bathtub"). The song appears again in Season 2, Chapter 8 ("The Mind Flayer) as Jonathan, Mike, Chief Hopper, and his mother Joyce attempt to communicate with Will through Morse code.

Just as Jonathan promised in Chapter 2, then, the song literally helps save Will's life—albeit in ways Jonathan probably did not foresee. On one level, the song's significance is familiarity—it anchors and comforts Will. It gives him something to hold onto, something that reminds him of family and friends.

It works the other way too—offering his family and friends evidence that he is still there, that he is not gone. The song, in this way, is like an interdimensional conduit. It communicates beyond language, space, and time.

Yet the song is not only used by Will to survive or even just to communicate with his family—but to communicate *something*. Listen to the lyrics:

> *Should I stay or should I go now?*
> *If I go, there will be trouble.*
> *And if I stay it will be double.*

That, in a nutshell, is Will's conundrum. When he goes, it causes trouble (his abduction emotionally devastates his family and friends, and turns the town of Hawkins upside down—pardon the pun). Yet when he is finally found at the end of Season 1 and returns home, that trouble—true to the song—only doubles, as the Upside Down spreads, the demodogs multiply, and the Mind Flayer threatens his—and everyone he loves'—existence.

It is revealing, though, that the song is what essentially allows him to subvert the Mind Flayer in Season 2, Chapter 8 ("The Mind Flayer"). It is not merely played by Jonathan for nostalgia; it helps him reconnect with his loved ones and deliver an important message (CLOSE GATE).

In this way, The Clash's hit track is not only part of the show's soundtrack, it is also deftly woven into its plot, themes, and characters. It symbolizes the brotherly bond between Jonathan and Will; it helps Will survive—and helps his family and friends keep hope alive—after he has been snatched into the Upside Down; and it underscores Will's paradoxical post-abduction plight, as he struggles to escape the grip of the Mind Flayer.

"Should I Stay or Should I Go" experienced a resurgence of popularity following its prominent role in the show. It also earned an Emmy nomination for music supervisor Nora Felder, who was somehow able to convince The Clash that the song should be featured in a show about extra-terrestrial monsters.

Fortunately, The Clash signed off. It is hard to imagine the show without the song. Yet there is a lot more great music in *Stranger Things* worth taking a closer look at, from pop classics to more obscure deep cuts. The '80s was an epic decade for music—from the synthesizers, to the music videos, to the gender bending. It was the decade of synth pop, new wave, hair metal, and hip hop. It was the decade of Michael Jackson and Madonna, Prince and The Police, U2 and Bruce Springsteen. That is a rich well from which to draw—and the show draws from it liberally to make both the period and story come to life.

Jonathan's Mix

How did the Duffer Brothers decide which songs to use for the show? "For us," explains Ross Duffer, "we didn't Tarantino it—it's not like this stuff was written in the script. The Clash's "Should I Stay or Should I Go?" was planned, but all the other stuff...it was more us listening to as much Eighties music as we could and seeing what hit the right mark. It was definitely trial and error. Obviously, we played around in terms of what would actually be played around 1983—for us, it was more about the tone and the feel, and the stories these songs were telling."

Stranger Things tends to cluster many of its songs around characters. For example, in addition to The Clash, a number of other punk, new wave, and alternative groups are featured in relation to Jonathan, from The Smiths "There Is a Light That Never Goes Out," which plays in one of Jonathan's flashbacks, to Reagan Youth's "Go Nowhere," which plays on his car stereo in Season 1, Chapter 2 ("The Weirdo on Maple Street").

One of the more poignant examples comes at the end of Chapter 3 ("Holly, Jolly"), in the first of a string of effective "mood songs" used in Season 1. In this case, the song is Peter Gabriel's cover of the David Bowie classic, "Heroes." We know, of course, that Jonathan is a huge Bowie fan—from his conversations with Will, to his mixtapes. There's even a poster of the pop icon on his bedroom wall.

Yet the use of the song here is not only about Jonathan, but about everyone who cared about Will. The song starts just as what seems to be the boy's lifeless body is being pulled out of the lake. We see Chief Hopper, stunned and somber; we see Will's friends looking on with tears; we see sons and mothers embracing. The song, and episode, end with Jonathan and Joyce holding onto each other, both nearly broken, in silhouette, as police sirens approach in the distance.

The Duffer Brothers credit producer Shawn Levy, who directed this episode, for picking the song and beautifully weaving it into these final, dramatic shots.

Another Jonathan Byers-culled mood song plays near the beginning of Chapter 4 ("The Body"). After Chief Hopper leaves the Byers house, they are left to digest the tragic news about Will. The song—Joy Division's B-side "Atmosphere"—accompanies a montage of grieving. We see Joyce wracked with pain but still refusing to accept that her son is gone. Jonathan, meanwhile, lays in his bed with headphones on, overwhelmed with sadness.

A requiem of loss and mourning, the song was originally released not long after the tragic death of Joy Division lead singer Ian Curtis in May 1980. Here, in *Stranger Things*, it allows the loss of Will, particularly to his mother and brother, fully sink in.

In Chapter 5 ("The Flea and the Acrobat"), we hear the haunting New Order instrumental, "Elegia," as we watch an emotional montage of Will's friends and family preparing for his funeral. New Order was formed after Joy Division lost its lead singer Curtis to suicide. Released on their studio album, *Low Life*, in 1985, "Elegia" was dedicated to Curtis's memory. In *Stranger Things*, as we listen to its prismatic synths and melancholy guitars, we see people going through the ritualistic routines of a funeral, before looking on at Will's casket, as a priest delivers a sermon. It is another powerful use of a piece of music to capture the devastation of losing a loved one.

We hear a number of other tracks that feel culled from Jonathan's playlists, including deep cuts like "Blackout" by Minnesota new wave band, Swing Set, and "Nocturnal Me," a dark, cinematic track by British rock band Echo & the Bunnymen. How did the Duffers rationalize a kid from small-town Indiana having such extensive knowledge of music? According to music supervisor Nora Felder, it was simply a natural extension of Jonathan's unique identity. "With his photography, he is always looking further to capture something unique and special through the lens," explains Felder. "It would only seem natural that he would also be curating his own personal music playlist and not relying on what's being fed to the town on the local radio station. Jonathan would surely what to know—no pun intended—'What else is out there?'"

By extension, Jonathan's mix—both the actual mixtapes he makes his brother Will as well as the music clearly connected to his tastes—introduces the audience to a wider palette of music, outside the bigger hits and superstars from the '80s. We get to hear groups like The Clash, Reagan's Youth, The Smiths, Joy Division, and New Order (music aficionados' fingers are still crossed for Talking Heads, The Cure, and R.E.M.).

Not that *Stranger Things* doesn't also give us more mainstream pop. For that, at least in part, we have Nancy and Steve to thank.

Pop Life

Throughout Season 1, the music accompanying Nancy and Steve sticks to more familiar pop fare—songs one undoubtedly would have heard on the radio in the '80s.

For example, in Season 1, Chapter 1 ("The Vanishing of Will Byers"), as Nancy and Steve's homework session turns into a makeout session we hear Toto's massive hit, "Africa." That track, in all of its cheesy, earnest, '80s glory, reached #1 in February of 1983 (the year Season 1 takes place). It has since become a pop culture favorite, featured on everything from *Community* to *The Tonight Show With Jimmy Fallon* (on which Fallon sings it with Justin Timberlake in a hilarious summer camp skit). Its appearance on *Stranger Things* effectively captures the relatively wholesome, vanilla charm of Steve and Nancy's relationship.

After Nancy and Steve take their relationship to the next level at his house in Chapter 2 ("The Weirdo on Maple Street"), we hear another big radio hit as the ending credits roll: the Bangles' cover of the Simon and Garfunkel classic, "Hazy Shade of Winter," which peaked at #2 in 1987 (some fans of the show noted it was one of several musical anachronisms—or creative liberties, depending on your point of view—since the song came out four years after Season 1 takes place). "Kind of a rule we had is that if it's a song a character is listening to in the show then it really needed to be from that era," explained Matt Duffer. "If it was just playing for the show then it was all about tone."

At the beginning of Chapter 3 ("Holly, Jolly"), meanwhile, as Nancy and Steve have sex for the first time, we hear Foreigner's power ballad, "Waiting for a Girl Like You," juxtaposed, ironically, with Barb being taken into the Upside Down. Well-played, Duffer Brothers. Foreigner's AOR (adult-oriented rock) staple spent a record ten weeks at the #2 spot on the Billboard Hot 100 through late 1981 and early 1982—held out of the top spot by Olivia Newton-John's aerobics anthem, "Physical." Nancy and Steve were probably not the only couple for whom the soft rock single was used to set the mood—although it obviously didn't work out as well for Barb.

The hits keep coming, it seems, every time Steve meets up with Nancy. In Chapter 2 ("The Weirdo on Maple Street"), while they chug beers and push each other in the pool, we hear Modern English's 1982 hit, "I Melt With You." In Chapter 6 ("The Monster"), Corey Hart's synth pop classic, "Sunglasses at Night," plays as Steve pulls up to the Wheeler's house and sneaks in Nancy's bedroom window, stealthy like a ninja. That song came out in the summer of 1984, receiving heavy radio airplay which propelled it into the Top Ten.

We hear another big hit in the first Chapter of Season 2 ("MADMAX") as Nancy and Steve discuss his paper—and future:

the Romantics' 1984 single, "Talking in Your Sleep." That song reached #3 in early 1984, the Romantics' biggest hit. There seems to be a bit of foreshadowing in the track as well, which is about unintentionally divulging secrets. It is the next episode when a plastered Nancy reveals to Steve that their state of denial about Barb—and relationship more generally—is "bullshit."

That episode, incidentally, also features Duran Duran's infamous classic, "Girls on Film." From the British band's debut self-titled album, the song announced Duran Duran as one of the biggest groups of the 1980s—although it has also become known as one of the more gratuitously misogynistic videos of the MTV era.

It's hard to tell if Steve has any favorite genres or artists, or if he simply sticks to what's on the radio. Somehow he seems like a Huey Lewis and the News kind of guy, though he might also be into 70s rock as we hear "Raise a Little Hell," by Canadian rock band Trooper, when he opens the door for Nancy and Barb in Season 1, Chapter 2 ("The Weirdo on Maple Street") and Queen's "Hammer to Fall" in Season 2, Chapter 6 ("The Spy") as he and Dustin prepare to check on D'Artagnan.

We get a better sense of Nancy's tastes as the show evolves, which, in addition to the more popular tunes, also contain some out-of-the-box surprises. For example, in her bedroom, instead of an artist one might expect—like Madonna—we see a poster of Debbie Harry from Blondie, an edgier choice that shows more independence than one might assume. During a phone conversation with Barb in Chapter 2 ("The Weirdo on Maple Street"), we also hear British new wave band Depeche Mode's "Enjoy the Silence"—which, granted, isn't nearly as out-of-the-box as some of Jonathan's favorites, but does put her closer to him in terms of preferences.

As the series progresses, the music reflects the changing dynamics of Nancy's relationships. In Season 2, Chapter 3 ("The Pollywog"), for example, after Nancy breaks up with Steve, we see

Jonathan and Nancy sitting on his car, having lunch at school, as the Psychedelic Furs' 1984 new wave ballad, "The Ghost in You," plays in the background. The lyrics describe finding someone who suddenly changes the way you experience the world. It coincides perfectly with Jonathan and Nancy's mutual confession about the losses they have experienced—and their recognition that they get each other in a way most do not.

The music, in between the alternative tastes of Jonathan and the more mainstream synth pop of Nancy, symbolizes the melding of their relationship. Tellingly, in the next episode, Chapter 4 ("Will the Wise"), after lying to her parents about where she will be that night, we hear the Clash's 1981 single, "This is Radio Clash," as Nancy walks out to meet Jonathan. In Chapter 5 ("Dig Dug"), likewise, as Nancy and Jonathan are pulling up at Murray Bauman's bunker, "Can Do What I Want," a song by electro-punk band Shock Therapy plays on the car stereo. Not only do these songs communicate her connection to Jonathan, they also express her growing rebellion and empowerment as she seeks to redress Barb's death.

Rock You Like a Hurricane

We are introduced to another strain of '80s music when we meet Billy in Season 2: heavy metal. As Billy pulls up in his California-plated Camaro and steps out in jean jacket and boots, the metal anthem "Rock You Like a Hurricane" accompanies his—and sister Max's—arrival in Hawkins. Released in 1984 by the German rock band, The Scorpions, "Rock You Like a Hurricane" remains a popular stadium anthem. It was in heavy rotation on MTV in the mid-'80s—part of a wave of hard rock and metal bands that also included AC/DC, Iron Maiden, Van Halen, Def Leppard, Poison, Guns N Roses, Metallica, and Motley Crue.

We hear a number of other metal tracks in relation to Billy throughout Season 2. For example, when he is driving with sister Max, complaining about Hawkins, in Chapter 2 ("Trick or Treat, Freak"), Ted Nugent's 1980 song, "Wango Tango," is playing. Later in that episode, at the Halloween party, as Billy demonstrates his kegging prowess, we hear the 1983 Motley Crue song, "Shout at the Devil." (At the same party, Jonathan sees a girl with black hair and makeup and mistakenly asks if she is dressed like a member from the famous glam rock band, Kiss—in fact, as Jonathan should know given his alternative aptitude, she is dressed as Siouxsie Sioux from Siouxsie and the Banshees).

We hear some deeper metal cuts as the season continues. In Season 2, Chapter 5 ("Dig Dug"), as Billy drops Max off at the arcade, "Metal Sport" blares from the car stereo, a song from obscure metal band Hittman. In Chapter 6 ("The Spy"), while he lifts weights at his house, he is listening to "Round and Round" by hair metal band Ratt as MTV plays on the TV. Billy's metal obsession is even evident in his room decor. On the wall, we see a poster of Metallica's 1983 album *Kill 'Em All.* We also see a poster for the more obscure British metal band Tank's 1982 album, *Filth Hounds of Hades* (which may also be a clever nod to the demodogs that begin to wreak havoc on Hawkins in Season 2).

Oldies

Most of the pre-'80s music in *Stranger Things* correlates with the adults. For example, when Chief Hopper walks into the police station in Season 1, Chapter 1 ("The Vanishing of Will Byers"), we hear "Can't Seem to Make You Mine," a 1966 song by the rock group The Seeds. In Season 2, Chapter 2 ("Trick or Treat, Freak") we get a better sense of Chief Hopper's musical tastes as he is flipping through his record collection at the old cabin. We see him pause on an album by '70s rock band Supertramp before settling on Jim Croce. "Alright, here we go," he says, before putting on Croce's 1972 track, "You Don't Mess Around With Jim." Hopper displays some classic dad dancing moves, before the pair get to work cleaning up the cabin.

In Season 2, we also get a pretty epic mix of lame parent music from Joyce's new boyfriend, Bob Newby. The generational contrast between Bob's tastes and Jonathan's tastes is highlighted in Chapter 1 ("MADMAX") when Jonathan is trying to convince Will that it's okay to be different and weird. "Who would you rather be? Bowie or Kenny Rogers," he asks. Will grimaces at the idea of Kenny Rogers. "Exactly," says Jonathan. "It's no contest." "Well," Will says, "some people like Kenny Rogers." Just as Will says it, Bob walks in. "I love Kenny Rogers!" The brothers laugh, as the unapologetically dorky (and endearing) Bob picks up a VHS rental of *Mr. Mom*—hooing with delight.

In the next episode ("Trick or Treat, Freak"), sure enough, we hear Bob listening to a Kenny Rogers duet with Dolly Parton, the 1983 classic, "Islands in the Stream," as he and Joyce slow-dance in the living room (incidentally, another Kenny Roger-Dolly Parton duet, "The Bargain Store," is playing when Nancy and Jonathan are getting supplies to kill the monster at the army surplus store in Season 1, Chapter 6 ("The Monster").

Karen Wheeler (played by Cara Buono) also brings some solid parent music to the table. In the Season 2 finale ("The Gate"), as she soaks in a bubble bath and reads a trashy romance novel, she is listening to "The Way We Were," Barbra Streisand's sappy ballad from the 1973 movie of the same name. Notably, the music gets a little more upbeat and current after Billy shows up. As she watches him take off in his Camaro, Donna Summer's "I Do Believe I Fell in Love" plays, the B-side to the 1983 hit, "She Works Hard For the Money."

Setting the Mood

There are some other great "mood songs" — songs that are less character-based, instead establishing a certain feel or tone — in the latter half of Season 1. For example, in Chapter 7 ("The Bathtub"), as the kids prepare the sensory deprivation pool in the Hawkins Middle School gymnasium, "Fields of Coral" plays by Vangelis. If that name isn't familiar, it certainly was in the '80s. A Greek composer who helped bridge the worlds of classical and electronic music, Vangelis created the iconic music for *Chariots of Fire* (1981), which won the Academy Award for Best Score, and *Blade Runner* (1982), one of the most popular science fiction soundtracks of all time. He also contributed the soundtrack to Carl Sagan's groundbreaking TV show, *Cosmos: A Personal Voyage* (explored more in Chapter 8).

In Chapter 8 ("The Upside Down"), meanwhile, we hear "Horizon" by Tangerine Dream, while Chief Hopper has a flashback to his daughter's battle with cancer. Like Vangelis, Tangerine Dream — an electronic group from Germany — helped revolutionize the sound of film music with synth-heavy, ambient scores. Among more than twenty films they contributed to in the '80s, were *Risky Business* (starring Tom Cruise) and *Firestarter* (the Stephen King adaptation starring Drew Barrymore). In *Stranger Things*, "Horizon" creates an ethereal intensity that not only captures the gravity of Hopper's loss, but also stresses the importance of the mission at hand.

Finally, there is Moby's "When It's Cold I'd like to Die," also in Chapter 8 ("The Upside Down") — this one featured in the dramatic scene when they find and resuscitate Will — which is juxtaposed with the final moments of his daughter Jane's life. One of only a handful of songs not from the '80s, "When It's Cold I'd like to Die" came out on the 1995 album, *Everything Is Wrong*, a relatively obscure collection of haunting, electronic-based songs. In *Stranger*

Things, it carries one of the more powerful scenes in Season 1, as the audience finally fills in the gaps from Hopper's past, and the relief of rescuing Will is subdued by another child that could not be saved. Such songs help give *Stranger Things* an emotional depth not found in many genre films.

The show, however, is just as effective at establishing upbeat tones. Obvious examples of this include "Ghostbusters" by Ray Parker, Jr. as the boys get ready for Halloween, as well as "Whip It" by the post-punk, new wave band Devo. The latter track, which plays as the boys pull up to the arcade in Season 2, Chapter 1 ("MADMAX"), was originally released in 1980 and became an unexpected hit due, in part, to its quirky music video, which became a staple of the early MTV era. The seemingly nonsensical lyrics satirize American optimism with a string of motivational clichés (inspired, in part, by novelist Thomas Pynchon). It fits the boys' quirky, outsider identities, while offering a feel of some of the unique, colorful sounds of the '80s.

Early in Season 2, we hear another "zeitgeist song"—a song that establishes a sense of the period and place— "Just Another Day" by Oingo Boingo, an American new wave band. The song plays to a montage of shots from around Hawkins—a woman jogging, a RadioShack, a theater marquee (featuring *The Terminator*), people heading to work. While "Just Another Day" was released in 1985, it feels right at home in the fall of 1984.

Finally, another important zeitgeist/character song comes in Season 2, Chapter 7 ("The Lost Sister"), as Eleven boards a bus to Chicago. The song: Bon Jovi's rock classic, "Runaway." A bit obvious, perhaps, but effective. That song was released in 1983, and became Bon Jovi's first Top 40 hit in 1984. In the show, of course, the song about a girl who feels trapped and ready to break out on her own, matches Eleven's state of mind. (Incidentally, the visuals in the scene also recall Pat Benatar's music video for "Love is a Battlefield" — a song featured later in the season).

The Holy Trinity of Pop

At least over its first two seasons, there has been no music in *Stranger Things* from the Holy Trinity of '80s pop: Michael Jackson, Prince, and Madonna. Given the subject matter of the show, it is particularly surprising that no Michael Jackson music has been featured since 1983-84 was the peak of *Thriller*-mania. Yet this absence seems to be more of a licensing issue than an oversight. As *Stranger Things* fans know, "Thriller" *was* used in the first promotional trailer for Season 2. It premiered at Comic-Con in San Diego and blew audiences away. It has since been watched over 15 million times on YouTube.

The Duffer Brothers had in mind to use the song for Season 2 from the get-go and "fell in love" with the trailer; however, getting the rights to use the song proved far trickier than they anticipated. "There's not been a trailer for any of my movies that I have obsessed over and gotten more personally hands-on over more than this 'Thriller' trailer," acknowledged producer Shawn Levy. Just weeks before Comic-con, recalls Levy, they had their "hearts shattered because we were told for a variety of reasons that ['Thriller'] was just not licensable." In its place, another trailer was created with different music and shipped to San Diego. "The [Duffer] brothers and I would watch it," recalls Levy, "and it really ate away at us, because we knew it was a good trailer, but with "Thriller" it's next level." So Levy refused to take no for an answer. He persisted, begged, cajoled, until he finally got the green light to use the track.

While there is no music from Jackson in the actual series, then, "Thriller" was at least featured in the trailer. Moreover, there seem to be a couple of subtle nods to the pop star in Season 2: the opening shot of the misty graveyard, including a skeleton hand reaching out from the ground, recalls the iconic visuals from "Thriller." In addition, a person at the Halloween party can be seen rocking Jackson's signature red jacket from "Billie Jean." We also see someone at that party dressed as Madonna, circa *Like a Virgin*. As for Prince, 1985 was the year his blockbuster album *Purple Rain* hit its peak, so perhaps we will hear something in Season 3.

The Snow Ball Playlist

The Hawkins Middle School Snow Ball is a great conclusion to Season 2 for a number of reasons. High on that list, however, has to be the selection of music. It begins with Pat Benatar's "Love is a Battlefield." The song plays, appropriately, as Steve is preparing Dustin for the emotional terrain of the school dance. Pat Benatar's song peaked at #5 on the Billboard Hot 100 in the fall of 1983 and earned the singer—a badass rocker who regularly featured on MTV in its early years—her fourth Grammy Award for Best Female Rock Vocal Performance.

Next up is a bright, synth pop cut—"Twist of Fate" by Olivia Newton-John. The song plays as Dustin makes his way into the dance, briefly exchanging pleasantries with Mr. Clarke ("thanks, my lord") and Nancy. "Twist of Fate" also reached #5 on the charts in late 1983, though it is less known by the average music listener. Featured in the 1983 romantic comedy *Two of a Kind* (which saw Newton-John reunite with actor John Travolta), the song was Newton-John's attempt to establish a hipper image following her goody-goody role as Sandy in *Grease* (1978). In addition to providing the right buoyant mood for the dance, it also seems to subtly foreshadow the twist of fate awaiting the characters in the days and months to come.

After Dustin finds his friends (and they give him a hard time about his Jheri curl/pompadour), the upbeat atmosphere of the dance suddenly slows down as Cyndi Lauper's classic synth pop ballad, "Time After Time," begins. Released as a single in early 1984, the song was Lauper's first #1 hit. It followed her generational anthem, "Girls Just Want to Have Fun," which peaked at #2. Both songs came from her 1983 album, *She's So Unusual*, an album that established Lauper as one of the era's most unique, quirky, and talented icons. "Time After Time" is one of her most enduring songs, still regularly receiving radio airplay and covered by numerous artists, from Miles Davis to Sarah McLaughlin. It was also, of course, a staple of school dances in the '80s, making it a perfect choice for the Snow Ball.

And finally, there is "Every Breath You Take," the most popular song of 1983—topping the charts for an incredible eight weeks—and one of the biggest hits of the decade. From the Police's final album, *Synchronicity*, the song, like "Time After Time," was in regular rotation at dances in the '80s—and continues to be popular today. In *Stranger Things*, it hits right at the climactic moment when Mike sees Eleven walk in.

However, in many ways, the song is darker than its tone suggests. Its songwriter, Sting, has repeatedly registered his bemusement at how often it is misinterpreted as a simple love song, when its lyrics communicate obsession, jealousy, surveillance, and control.

The Duffer Brothers, however, were aware of this and perfectly utilize the song's paradoxical nature. We first hear it as a simple love song at a dance; but as it continues, and we move outside the glittery confines of the gymnasium, the camera gradually begins to tilt. *"Oh, can't you see...you belong to me..."* The music begins to fade and is finally swallowed, as we find ourselves looking at a much darker version of Hawkins Middle School—in the Upside Down. Above it now is an ominous red sky, thunder and lightning, and the

Mind Flayer, ominously enveloping the building. Suddenly, the lines of Police's hit song—"every step you take, every breath you take, I'll be watching you"—aren't so innocuous.

"We always wanted to get that [song] in there," acknowledged Matt Duffer. "It felt like it worked for the romantic part, but also there's something creepy about the song—"I'll be watching you"—that led into our final reveal of the Mind Flayer over the gym. This is something that's still there, still watching them. I like that it had kind of a dual meaning. I'd just been trying to find a place for that song since season one, so I really wanted it. Netflix was passionate and really wanted it in, too. It was not super-cheap, but I'm glad we got it in there."

Given how deftly the show incorporates music—from "Should I Stay Or Should I Go" to "Waiting For a Girl Like You"—it is a perfect way to end the season, with the music operating as both soundtrack and subtext.

5

Childhood

There's something about that moment in Season 1, Chapter 1 ("The Vanishing of Will Byers"), when the kids are leaving the house. It's night. They've just finished playing Dungeons & Dragons in Mike's basement. The shimmering synth soundtrack kicks in (the Kyle Dixon and Michael Stein composition, "Kids"). They get on their bikes with homemade flashlights. And they ride off together, into the dark suburban streets.

No helmets. No parents. Just kids.

You can practically feel the cool night air as they bike through the neighborhood — that rush, that elation. That freedom.

That's the first thing that comes to mind for many who grew up as kids in the '80s: freedom. Riding bikes to school (without parent supervision). Heading to a friend's house (without parent supervision). Going to the mall or the playground or pool, maybe even the cemetery at night (without parent supervision). Sure, we'd check in now and then. Most kids had curfews (although it was common to sneak out at night). But there were hours each day that belonged to us. We explored. We did things we shouldn't. We operated off-radar. Adults had their own lives; we had ours.

This is not just nostalgia. Studies back it up. In the 1980s, over seventy percent of kids walked or biked to school without parents, many as early as kindergarten. Today, that number is under ten percent. There was no pick-up protocol at most schools. When school was dismissed, kids went where they went. The idea seems bizarre by today's standards. But pick any activity—going to the playground, to baseball practice, to the movie theater—and more kids, by far, were doing it without supervision in the '80s than they are today.

Many Millennials and Gen-Zers love *Stranger Things* precisely because of this unstructured, unsupervised version of childhood it represents. Asked about what felt different about going back to that time period as an actor, Millie Bobby Brown (Eleven) responded: "I think it was the freedom. Because they had so much freedom back then and I'm very limited in my freedom now, because I can't go outside without my mom literally standing right beside me."

Millie is not alone. Millennials and Gen-Zers, statistically, are far more closely supervised than their predecessors. They are much more likely to be dropped off and picked up from activities. They are much less likely to hang out at each other's houses on a whim. Their locations and movements are often tracked via smartphones, smartwatches, or other devices. Parents almost always know exactly where their kids are.

That wasn't the case in the 1980s—the world re-created for us in *Stranger Things*. According to the Duffers, the show simply wouldn't have worked if it was set in the present because it depends on that childhood freedom and mystery. "We grew up without cell phones," explains Ross Duffer. "I don't know what it's like growing up now, but when we were kids, you'd go outside, you'd go into the woods behind your house, and your parents [couldn't] contact you. They don't know where you are. There was this sense of, 'What if we find a treasure map out here, and mobsters were after us, and we'd find a ship with gold?' It feels like now, your mom texts you that it's time for dinner—it might just take you right out of that."

Kids in the '80s—untethered by cell phones, blocked-out schedules, and helicopter parents—were free to move about suburbs and cities alike with remarkable latitude.

Of course, it's easy to romanticize the past. Some may view such laxity, by today's standards, as neglect—perhaps even irresponsible and dangerous. Even at the time, there were growing concerns. Some kids resented their parents' lack of attention. The culture at large was anxious about changing family dynamics. Divorce and single-parent homes were on the rise, as were the amount of families with two working parents, leading to a generation of so-called "latchkey kids": a term applied to children who returned from school to empty homes because parents were still at work. The '80s also marked the beginning of a national panic about child abduction—which is, in many ways, responsible for the massive sea change that has led us to where we are today.

Which is to say that even in the 1980s, people weren't in agreement about how children were growing up, or how parents were parenting. But it is this period-specific iteration of childhood—and its percolating tensions between freedom and fear—that is represented so authentically in *Stranger Things*.

Bikes

Perhaps the ultimate symbol of childhood freedom from the '80s is the bike. The bike allowed kids mobility: not only could they go places, they could get there relatively fast, and without depending on adults. In this way, a bike offered children a sense of control and empowerment; it gave them an early sense of being able to navigate and explore the world on their own.

As in many other classic '80s movies—*E.T.*, *The Goonies*—bikes play a crucial role in *Stranger Things*. "Bikes," notes television critic Glen Weldon, "allow the kids to slip between the cracks and explore on their own, beyond adult attention. So important are they to this form of storytelling that the discovery of one kid's abandoned bike is the trigger that first alerts *Stranger Things'* sheriff that something isn't right." Indeed, when Chief Hopper finds Will's bike in the woods in Season 1, Chapter 1 ("The Vanishing of Will Byers"), he can't imagine Will not bringing it home under normal circumstances." A bike like this is like a Cadillac to these kids," he tells his deputies.

Hopper's remark highlights the significance of the bike to a child in the '80s—especially a BMX bike like Will's. The popularity of the BMX bike exploded in the '80s. An outgrowth of the 1970s dirt bike scene in Southern California, BMXs soon became ubiquitous in youth culture. Unlike most bikes for kids before them, they were stylized and tough—intended for stunts and off-road driving. They were also easy to customize. Freestyle BMX biking reached its peak of popularity in the mid-'80s. Not only were they featured in major blockbuster films like *E.T.*, they were also the inspiration for movies like *BMX Bandits* (1983) and *Rad* (1986). BMX bikes were synonymous with cool; owning one became an extension of a kid's identity, much like Nikes would later in the decade.

Prop master Lynda Reiss went to great lengths to find the right bikes for the boys in *Stranger Things*. She needed sixteen bikes in all—one primary, one backup, one stunt bike, and one backup stunt bike for each kid. Since it was difficult to find that many bikes of the same style, Reiss went with a mixture of banana-seat bikes and BMX bikes. "Mike's bike is actually a reproduction," Reiss says. "We aged them all up and taped them. With Dustin's bike, we decided he was sort of a klutz. So we painted his bike but never finished it, and that's why his bike is two colors."

Those bikes make an appearance in just about every episode of *Stranger Things*. Perhaps the most memorable scene, however, comes in Season 1, Chapter 7 ("The Bath"). The episode opens as Eleven and Mike are having a moment. Just as they seem to be about to kiss for the first time, however, Dustin suddenly barges in the room, shouting that Lucas is in trouble. Through a weak, muffled signal on the walkie talkie, he warns that the "bad men are coming." They need to leave now.

The kids run upstairs, look out the window, and discover that, sure enough, the Wheeler house is surrounded by white vans, labeled "Hawkins Power and Light." Mike tries to get information from his mom (*did she call about repairs?!*), but she's on the phone, too preoccupied to understand the urgency of his question.

"If anyone asks where I am," Mike declares to his baffled mom, "I've left the country." With that, he bolts out the side door with Eleven and Dustin, where the bikes lie waiting for their great escape.

As the kids stealthily run their bikes across the lawn, they are spotted by agents from Hawkins Lab, including Dr. Brenner. "Go! Go! Go!" Dustin yells. Eleven hops on the back of Mike's banana seat; Dustin on his haphazardly painted BMX.

The kids begin navigating an intricate suburban grid of secret pathways, backyards, and side alleys, trying to elude the white vans. Coordinating via Walkie Talkies, they eventually meet up with Lucas, assuming they have lost the Hawkins Lab agents. Just when they think they are safe, however, they see the white vans again and the chase resumes.

The chase is undoubtedly the best cinematic bike sequence since *E.T.* Indeed, in many ways it is a direct homage to the famous scene from Spielberg's film. The Duffer Brothers told *Entertainment*

Weekly that they "originally did not have a bike chase planned for this season," fearing it would be viewed as derivative. "We tried to resist the impulse, we honestly did," they acknowledged. "But we're only human."

Thankfully they gave in—not only is the bike chase among the most exciting five minutes of the season, it also created one of the show's most iconic moments. Everyone remembers the famous moment in *E.T.* when the kids on bikes, seemingly trapped by a blockade of police cars, suddenly fly up over the top, as John Williams' score makes the audience feel every ounce of their surprise and elation.

Stranger Things cleverly draws on and inverts this moment. As in *E.T.*, the kids manage to elude the Lab agents, before finding themselves trapped on both sides. Just as the van in front of them is closing in, Eleven lowers her head and flips it with her mind. Instead of the kids flying over the blockade, the van goes airborne.

We see this incredible moment from three different angles: first, from straight on, making it feel as if the van is heading directly at the audience; then from the side in slow motion, capturing the sense of shock and awe as the van suddenly elevates above them; and finally, looking down from above, showing the kids' stunned expressions as the vehicle flips over their heads.

As the van crashes down behind them, obstructing the other vehicles, the kids keep riding, looking back as if to confirm that what just happened just happened. The Hawkins Lab agents seem equally astounded, including Dr. Brenner, who seems more impressed than angry.

Bikes, then, are not only a symbol of childhood freedom; they allow the kids to elude danger and outmaneuver adults (with a little help from Eleven's superpowers, of course).

Fittingly, the cover art for *Stranger Things* features Lucas, Dustin, and Mike on their bikes. Netflix commissioned British artist

Kyle Lambert to paint the very '80s-esque photorealistic character collage. Lambert was inspired by the poster art of Drew Struzan, who created the famous covers for the the *Star Wars* trilogy and *Blade Runner*. Lambert wanted the *Stranger Things* poster, like the posters for those classics, to tell a story—to capture the characters, symbols, and motifs that mattered most to the series. Right in the center of that collage is the ultimate emblem of childhood in the '80s: kids on bikes.

Missing Children

Incidentally, when the Duffer Brothers originally pitched *Stranger Things*, they also featured the bike as the central image—in this early phase, not an elaborate collage, but a simple, stripped-down image of Will's abandoned bike. "We literally took the *Firestarter* paperback [Stephen King's 1980 novel] and pasted a picture of a bike on top of it and changed the font to our font," recalls Matt Duffer.

That more minimalist focus on the abandoned bike points to one of the show's other main plot points and themes: the fear of a disappearing child. The '80s gave rise to a national panic about childhood safety and "stranger danger" that irrevocably transformed American culture.

This panic began with a handful of high-profile disappearances. In 1979, Etan Patz, a six-year-old boy from New York, was kidnapped on his way to school. His mysterious disappearance riveted the public and, with the efforts of his father (a professional photographer with media connections), quickly turned into a local and then national media frenzy.

Other high-profile cases followed: in 1981, Adam Walsh, son of John Walsh, who later became the famed host of *America's Most Wanted*, was kidnapped at a Sears in Florida. It was subsequently discovered that he was murdered. His story received an enormous amount of press and was eventually turned into a made-for-TV movie in 1983.

The early '80s also saw the Terror in Atlanta (or Atlanta Child Murders), in which dozens of kids, mostly black boys from inner-city Atlanta, went missing from 1979-1981. In all, at least 28 young people attached to the case were discovered dead. The Atlanta Child Murders received saturation coverage in the news media, and later spawned a major TV miniseries in 1985.

The outcry from such incidents created the so-called "missing child movement," and eventually led to new legislation (congress passed the Missing Children's Act in 1982) and protocols for dealing with child abduction (including the first nationwide tracking efforts).

In the early '80s, missing children began appearing on milk cartons—an attempt to alert the public to be on the lookout. Missing children also began appearing on pizza boxes and mailers, often with the simple question: *Have you seen me?* In 1983, the year Season 1 of *Stranger Things* takes place, President Ronald Reagan designated the four-year anniversary of Etan Patz's disappearance (May 25th) as National Missing Children's Day. The next year the National Center for Missing and Exploited Children was created. Meanwhile, each night, just before the local news, a public service announcement intoned, "It's 10pm. Do you know where your children are?"

The result of all of these efforts, ironically, was not a greater sense of security, but a heightened state of fear and anxiety. As Paula Fuss writes in her book, *Kidnapped: Child Abduction in America*, "Eventually, as kidnapping rang louder and louder cultural alarms about childhood danger, no child was safe." Paradoxically, that is, the "more we know about the crime and the more fearsome it becomes, the more addicted we become to the dangers it poses for the children we love."

It wasn't just kidnappings that gripped public attention in the '80s either: there were also panics about sexual abuse, daycare facilities, the safety of playground equipment, the impacts of cable television and music and video games...the list goes on and on. If the bike symbolized childhood freedom, the abandoned bike—and Will's disappearance—represents this growing fear: that something menacing might be lurking just around the corner, ready to snatch up the innocent.

Family Matters

Will's disappearance—as well as Barb's—in *Stranger Things* is perfectly in tune with this anxiety-filled zeitgeist. Yet it also demonstrates that parents hadn't quite transformed into the helicopter parents of today.

Will is a textbook definition of a latchkey child. His father, Lonnie, is mostly out of the picture. His mother, Joyce, is a single parent. She works full-time as a retail clerk. She doesn't realize Will is missing until the following morning. Her older son, Jonathan was supposed to be in charge of him while she worked a late shift (Jonathan was also responsible for waking him up and getting him off to school the next morning). Jonathan, however, was working late too, and assumed Will would be fine with his friends. Such arrangements were not out of the ordinary for families in the 1980s.

Divorce rates nearly doubled in the 1960s and 70s. They reached their historical peak in 1981, at which point nearly 50% of all marriages ended in divorce. That meant a lot of single parent homes like the Byers. It also meant a lot of latchkey kids like Jonathan and Will. Given the context, it makes sense that Will would come home late from a friend's house by himself—and that he would come back to an empty house. Even when his mother finds him missing, it still seems reasonable that he simply spent the night at the Wheeler's house.

Such lack of supervision wasn't unique to single-parent homes. Even though their house is the friend-hub, the Wheeler parents are frequently in the dark about their kids' activities and whereabouts. In the first few episodes, they have no idea that the kids have been playing Dungeons & Dragons for ten uninterrupted hours; they have no idea Nancy is dating Steve, or that he sneaks into her room at night; and they have no idea that Mike is hiding Eleven in their basement.

This isn't to say they are terrible parents. Karen clearly cares about her children. She consoles Mike when Will goes missing, and tries to get Nancy to open up about what's going on in her life. In Chapter 3 ("Holly, Jolly"), after Nancy spends the night at Steve's house, she pleads with her daughter to be honest with her: "You can talk to me," she says. "You can talk to me." But Nancy, like many teenagers, resists confiding in her mom. Eventually, she does admit that she slept with Steve and that something happened to Barb; however, she keeps most of what she is doing and experiencing over the first two seasons secret. That turns out to be quite a bit.

The Byers and Wheelers, as families, are relatable precisely because of these authentic dynamics. Joyce may not be always be there for her kids, but she's trying. She knows people will judge her for Will's disappearance, but rather than dwell on other's perceptions she goes into overdrive to find him. In Season 1, Chapter 1 ("The Vanishing of Will Byers"), she also acknowledges that she hasn't always been there for Jonathan. "I've been working so hard and I just feel bad," she says. "I barely know what's going on with you. I'm sorry."

This absence isn't without context. In the next episode ("The Body"), we learn that she has worked overtime and holidays to try to make ends meet for her two boys. When Will goes missing, she sacrifices everything to find him, refusing to back down when just about everyone around her think she's crazy. In Season 1, Chapter 4 ("The Body"), Jonathan acknowledges to Hopper that his mom has struggled with mental health issues in the past. He knows she isn't perfect, but he is mature enough to recognize what she's been through, and how hard she's tried. "My mom," he tells Hopper. "She's tough."

As for the Wheelers, they are in many ways more dysfunctional than the Byers—a refreshing subversion of stereotypes often associated with single-parent homes versus two-parent homes. The Wheelers may be better off financially and eat dinner together, but they struggle just the same. As Matt Duffer explains, "Yes, they seem like they're the perfect family, but they're certainly not. Ted is far from the best dad ever, and Karen is very overwhelmed. It's almost like there's this façade of a perfect life and a perfect stable family, and I think that's kind of what Jonathan tries to drive home for Nancy."

Nancy knows that her parents' marriage is strained—in fact, she openly questions whether they married for love in the first place. That may or may not be a fair judgment. But there are definitely breakdowns in communication. In Chapter 1 ("The Vanishing of Will Byers"), for example, family dinner quickly deteriorates, causing both Nancy and Mike to storm off to their rooms and prompting Karen to deliver one of the funnier lines of the season ("I hope you're enjoying your chicken, Ted").

As for Ted (played by Joe Chrest), he perfectly embodies the aloof, clueless, conservative middle class father. He is not mean or stern; but he is also not very present or perceptive as a husband or father (to the chagrin of his wife). The most he gets after his kids is with a boilerplate sports analogy or an obligatory, *"Language!"* when someone curses. Most of the time when we see him he is either napping on his recliner, watching TV, or reluctantly answering the door (no wonder Karen is often seen with a glass of wine).

When the Hawkins agents descend on his house in Season 1, Chapter 7 ("The Bathtub"), Ted scoffs at the idea that Mike would be hiding Eleven in the house. "Our son with a girl?" he says. "Believe me, if he had a girl sleeping in this house we'd know about it." He pauses for a moment, then looks at his wife. "Wouldn't we?"

The irony is not only that Mike has in fact been hiding a girl in their basement—or that Nancy has had Steve in her room—but how little he knows about his children in general. This is driven home, to comedic effect, in Season 2, Chapter 5 ("Dig Dug"), when Dustin drops by. Dustin asks if Mike is home, and as usual, Ted has to ask his wife. Karen, who is on the phone, shouts that he is at Will's. Dustin then asks if Nancy is there, and Ted again asks his wife, who again shouts that she is at a friend's house. "Our children don't live here anymore," Ted says, "Didn't you know that?"

Mike and Nancy, then, are as much latchkey kids as Will and Jonathan, if not more so. The Wheeler parents may be home more often, but, as Ted admits, they know very little about what's actually going on in their kids' lives. Not that Mike and Nancy seem to mind. They've got their own concerns.

In the latter half of Season 2, Nancy attempts to discover and expose the secrets of Hawkins Lab with Jonathan, as Mike tries to help Will resist being overcome by the Mind Flayer. Meanwhile, in the climactic Chapter 9 "(The Gate"), we see Ted asleep in his La-Z-boy recliner, while Karen is unwinding in a bubble bath, surrounded by candles, reading the kind of mass-market erotic romance novel one might find in the grocery store checkout aisle. Such books were enormously popular among suburban mothers in the '80s, bored by the mundane routines of their day-to-day lives.

Karen's temporary escape is memorably disrupted by the doorbell. Her husband, of course, doesn't hear it—or her screaming at him to answer it. So she puts on her bathrobe and rushes downstairs. At the door, it turns out, is chest-baring, baritone-voiced Billy Hargrove, looking for his sister Max. The sexual tension between Billy and Karen is played up Mrs. Robinson-style for comedic effect. Billy is like a character torn straight out of the forbidden fantasies of her romance novel: sexy, dangerous, not Ted.

Yet his visit also reminds—once again—that she and her husband don't have a clue where their children are. "If you see Mike," she says to Billy, "tell him to come home." Mike (and Nancy), at this point, are together at the Byers house—after encountering adventures and dangers their parents could not possibly imagine.

Sure, the gap between the kids and parents may be a bit exaggerated. But it's familiar enough to resonate for those who grew up in the era. Parents in the '80s—for better or worse—simply did not feel obligated to know where there kids were all the time.

Being Kids

Yet even in *Stranger Things*, one can sense certain changes emerging. After what happened to her son in Season 1, Joyce becomes much more cautious and protective. In Season 2, she drops Will off at the arcade, rather than allowing him to ride his bike like the other boys. She has Bob take him to school. And she asks Jonathan to accompany him trick-or-treating.

Still, even with these efforts to keep a closer eye on him, Will still has quite a bit of freedom: there is no adult watching him at the arcade; he is still allowed to do after-school activities like the AV Club; and Jonathan decides to let him go trick-or-treating without supervision.

The Byers family, in this way, is fairly representative of the country more broadly in the '80s. Fears about child safety were growing in the wake of high-profile abductions; but parents, by and large, still allowed their kids quite a bit of latitude compared to today. And for those who were more strict—like Chief Hopper with Eleven—kids often still found ways to venture outside the purview of their parents or guardians.

Which is not completely different than parent-child dynamics today. Yet there is an undeniable distance (and appeal) to the less structured, more adventurous iteration of childhood represented in *Stranger Things*. There were dangers then as there are dangers now. The show recognizes some of these dangers. Its vision of childhood is not without risks and threats, some familiar, some supernatural.

But that childhood freedom—hiding out in forts for hours, walking down train tracks, exploring scary places, riding bikes, alone, without grownups—is as much a part of life in the '80s as the music or the movies.

6

The Reagan Era

S_tranger Things_ 2 begins on October 28, 1984, less than two weeks before the presidential election.

That election pitted Republican incumbent Ronald Reagan against former Democratic Vice President Walter Mondale. Reagan was the heavy favorite. His first term in office had been turbulent: his popularity soared to over 60% after surviving a failed assassination attempt by John Hinckley, Jr. in 1981, but by late 1982, that number had dropped to under 40% as Reaganomics—the nickname for the president's trickle down economic policies—seemed to have failed and America was mired in a deep recession.

By 1983, however, there were indications of a recovery. Inflation was down; employment was up. As 1984 rolled around, the United States was gearing up for the Olympics in Los Angeles, the stock market was soaring, and the economy was getting back on track. It was perfect timing for Reagan's reelection. His approval numbers were back in the mid-50s—and his now-iconic campaign commercials, steeped in wholesome values, nostalgia, and nationalism—claimed it was "Morning in America."

After the first presidential debate that fall, the polls tightened as questions were raised about Reagan's age and mental acuity. But on November 6, 1984, America voted for Reagan in a landslide—one of the largest landslides in American history. Reagan carried 49 of 50 states (losing only Minnesota), and winning 525 of the 538 total electoral votes.

We see indications of the presidential election sprinkled throughout Hawkins, Indiana. At Hawkins Middle School, a sign reads, "Vote Here, Nov. 6." We also see yard signs, most of which show support for Reagan-Bush (particularly in the wealthier Loch Nora neighborhood), including one on the front lawn of the Wheeler house. This is not surprising. Reagan not only carried the national vote in a landslide; he won historically conservative Indiana with 62% of the vote, compared to just 38% for Mondale.

The only county in the state Reagan lost was Lake County, a predominantly African American county on the northern border of the state, near Chicago. There is no clear indication of which candidate Lucas's family voted for, or the Byers, for that matter. We do see a Mondale-Ferraro sign, however, outside Dustin's home, indicating that the Hendersons are one of the few Hawkins families publicly going against the grain and voting for the Democratic ticket.

We see a handful of other Reagan references throughout the first couple of seasons of *Stranger Things*. In Season 1, Chapter 3 ("Holly, Jolly"), as Chief Hopper and his officers approach Hawkins Laboratory, they allude to Reagan's "Star Wars" program—the nickname for the president's controversial Cold War strategic defense initiative, which was intended to protect against potential attacks from the Soviet Union.

Later in that same episode, as Eleven is flipping through channels on TV, she sees President Reagan giving a speech on the Beirut, Lebanon bombing in 1983. That attack—considered the first major terrorist act against America—left 241 U.S. service personnel (mostly Marines) and 58 French soldiers dead. President Reagan described the attack as a "brutal massacre" and pledged to keep a military presence in Lebanon; however, by 1984, he had second thoughts and ordered the withdrawal of all U.S. troops from Lebanon.

More than just a few random references, however, *Stranger Things* takes place within the cultural and ideological contours of the Reagan era. What does that mean? It means the show does a great job balancing the period's charms and virtues with its darker undercurrents.

Upside Down

There are no serious indications of poverty, crime, or blight in Hawkins, Indiana. In most ways, it resembles Reagan's "Morning in America" ad: a nostalgic celebration of middle-class suburbia. Sure, there are class differences—the Byers' house, more run-down and rural, falls in notable contrast to the Wheelers' neatly manicured two-story home in Loch Nora. But prior to Will and Barb's disappearances, Hawkins seems like a pretty typical, small, sleepy, safe American town. Probably a bit too safe and self-enclosed, if you asked Jonathan Byers.

Jonathan plays many roles in *Stranger Things*: big brother, replacement father figure, Nancy's eventual love interest, music aficionado. Yet his character is also important for giving us an alternative viewpoint on the era. Jonathan's disillusionment is not just personal; it's political. We see this early in Season 1, perhaps most prominently through his music.

In Chapter 2 ("The Weirdo on Maple Street"), before the Clash's "Should I Stay or Should I Go" plays on his drive to visit his father, we hear the end of punk rock band Reagan Youth's "Go Nowhere." Reagan's Youth's name was a riff on Hitler Youth, the tyrant's organization for young Germans, infamous for its blind allegiance to the Nazi regime. The band's music was brash and provocative, frequently taking aim at the Reagan Administration and the decade's greed and hypocrisy more broadly.

The song Jonathan is listening to conveys a sense of alienation that resonated for the non-Yuppie contingent of his generation (Generation X), questioning the point of living the typical suburban script. As the lyrics put it: "A whole generation of gonowheres/The living dead in 3-D life/A whole generation of stagnant lives."

Jonathan's worldview also comes through in some of his conversations. He routinely reminds his younger brother Will that it's okay to be different and not conform to society's expectations.

In Season 1, Chapter 5 ("The Flea and the Acrobat"), Jonathan delivers a piercing critique of Nancy (prompted by her similarly piercing critique of him). He was starting to think she was different, he says, and "not just another suburban girl who thinks she's rebelling by doing exactly what every other suburban girl does—until that phase passes and they marry some boring one-time jock who now works sales and they live out a perfectly boring life at the end of a cul-de-sac, exactly like their parents, who they thought were so depressing, but now, hey, I get it." Jonathan's rant isn't entirely fair to Nancy, who later proves far more independent than he gives her credit for. But it does highlight his general distaste for phoniness and conformity, which he believes is rampant in Hawkins, Indiana.

In Chapter 2 ("The Weirdo on Maple Street"), Jonathan's estranged father Lonnie suggests that he get out of Hawkins (which he describes as a "hell hole") and move to the city, where people are more "real." Jonathan may indeed fit in better in an urban environment. Yet when we finally get a taste of life outside of Hawkins in Season 2, Chapter 7 ("The Lost Sister"), it's clear that cities, particularly in the Reagan era, had their problems as well.

On the one hand, Eleven's arrival in Chicago is exciting—bright lights; big buildings; new, interesting people. Yet as she makes her way through the city we also see rampant homelessness, poverty, and drug abuse. The Duffers were inspired by the tone and feel of some of the more stylized, gritty, urban-based films of the '80s, including James Cameron's *The Terminator* (1984) and Tim Burton's *Batman* (1989). The latter film's Gotham City was particularly influential. "You've got steam coming out of the ground," explains Matt Duffer, "and you've got dirty homeless people shouting at the camera in trench coats. It was a very specific feeling that I wanted to evoke."

In this way, the episode also highlights the deterioration of cities during the Reagan era—which came to be referred to as "urban decay." Increasingly, as the wealthy fled to the suburbs, inner-cities were left underfunded and riddled with crime, drugs, and violence. It was the era of the crack epidemic and record-high homicide rates. Parts of major midwest cities like Chicago, Cleveland, and Detroit seemed to be crumbling as tens of thousands of manufacturing jobs disappeared.

Still, amidst the broken glass, abandoned buildings, dirty streets, and graffiti, some vibrant subcultures thrived, including the punk and hip hop scenes. Kali's gang—a diverse crew of outcasts residing in an industrial warehouse —embodies this countercultural strain. Sure, they're a bit cartoonish. But they are intended to represent resistance and retribution—to those who have wronged them individually, but more broadly at those responsible for perpetuating inequality and injustice. They are the avenging angels of the Reagan era.

On a more symbolic level, the Upside Down can also be read as the darker underbelly of the idyllic surface of the Reagan era. From one vantage point, everything seems relatively normal and tranquil. But lurking just beneath that surface is rot and terror, destruction and death. It is not so different than, for example, the Terror in Atlanta, in which the shiny image of a "city too busy to hate" was shattered when over twenty-eight young black children and teens were abducted and murdered in just two years (1979-1981).

Ronald Reagan described the Atlanta child murders as "one of the most tragic situations" ever to confront an American community. But it didn't occur in a vacuum; rather, it was the result of conditions that, as author James Baldwin put it, "did not so much alter the climate of Atlanta as reveal, or, as it were, epiphanize it." The Upside Down, than, can be interpreted not just as a nightmarish alternate dimension, but as the flip side of America, the darker side— which was often hidden or ignored—in narratives of the optimistic '80s.

One Step Ahead of the Russians

Another looming concern in the '80s was the looming prospect of nuclear war with the Soviet Union. In the early '80s, in particular, Reagan's confrontational language and aggressive policies had many concerned we were on the brink of disaster. The policy of Mutual Assured Destruction meant that the US and Soviet Union relentlessly sought the upper-hand in nuclear strength, foreign intelligence, and military sophistication. During the so-called Arms Race, billions of dollars and over 70,000 nuclear bombs were created in an attempt to maintain superiority in the event of a nuclear showdown.

Cold War anxiety permeated the '80s. In the fall of 1983, the made-for-TV movie, *The Day After*, depicted a nuclear holocaust between the US and Soviet Union so disturbing that ABC and local TV affiliates opened 1-800 hotlines with counselors on-call for distressed viewers. Even President Reagan wrote in his diary that watching the movie left him "greatly depressed" and made him rethink his strategy with the Soviet Union. The movie was watched by over 100 million people—the most watched TV movie in history—indicative of how much the prospect of a nuclear armageddon concerned Americans the year *Stranger Things* begins.

In this context, the purpose of Hawkins National Laboratory makes more sense. A mysterious federal complex on the fringe of town surrounded by barbed wire fences and guarded by military police, most residents in Hawkins are oblivious to its true activities. Most assume it is simply an energy facility responsible for power and electricity. There are rumors, however, among the more inquisitive, that more is going on in there. As they enter the facility, Callahan, one of Chief Hopper's officers, says that he's heard they "make space weapons in there."

In Chapter 3 ("Holly, Jolly"), when Chief Hopper investigates the Lab for information about Will, he prods a representative about what goes on inside the facility. "Trying to stay one step ahead of the Russians?" "I expect something like that," the representative responds. Hopper is subsequently shown surveillance tapes of the night Will went missing. The only problem: they have been doctored. The night Will disappeared there was a rainstorm, but in the tapes Hopper is shown there is no rain, tipping him off to the fact that the Lab has something to hide.

In Season 1, Hawkins National Laboratory is run by Dr. Martin Brenner (played by Matthew Modine). A sinister, grey-haired figure, Brenner is a research scientist who has presumably been given permission to conduct a range of unorthodox, clandestine experiments in the name of national defense. Gradually, through Eleven's flashbacks, we get a better sense of what those experiments are and what the real mission is inside the Lab's imposing walls.

Eleven, we learn, was, in essence, a human guinea pig, taken from her mother at birth because of her rare psychokinetic abilities. Instead of a real name, she was given a number, "011," and instead of a real home, she was raised in Hawkins Laboratory, where her development—and that of others—was overseen by Dr. Brenner.

Brenner serves as a sort of father figure to Eleven (she refers to him as "Papa"); yet his primary objective is to train, test, and expand her abilities. Thus, in flashbacks, we see her evolve from crushing Coke cans to crushing people. For any failure or non-cooperation she is put in solitary confinement. She is, as Eleven's aunt, Becky Ives, puts it, not thought of as a human being, but as a weapon for "fightin' the commies."

We see how that plays out, at least in part, in Chapter 4 ("The Body"), when Eleven is ordered by Dr. Brenner to spy on a Soviet agent and repeat what she hears. He shows her a photo of the agent as a terrified Eleven, wearing a head-scanning device and hospital gown, listens. Dr. Brenner then puts his hand on the back of her neck, as she focuses in on the photo, closes her eyes, and mind-travels to a white-tiled room. There, she finds the Soviet agent and begins broadcasting his remarks over the Lab's speakers.

Conspiracy Theories

While the audience learns more about the actives in Hawkins Lab through Eleven's flashbacks, a number of other characters begin gleaning more information through their own investigations into the disappearances of Will and Barb. In Chapter 3 ("Holly, Jolly"), Chief Hopper and Officer Powell make a trip to the library to search newspaper archives related to Hawkins National Laboratory. The facility, he discovers, has a long, disturbing history. We see headlines like "Hawkins Lab Blocks Inquiry," "Dr. Martin Brenner Named in Lawsuit," and "MKUltra Exposed." The articles describe a range of inhumane activities—including experimental drug tests, mind control, and accidental deaths—conducted covertly under the auspices of the CIA. It also tips Hopper off to a woman named Terry

Ives, a participant in the experiments who filed a lawsuit against Dr. Brenner, claiming he kidnapped her daughter, Jane (Eleven), for scientific research.

After reading the articles, Chief Hopper is convinced the Lab is implicated in the disappearance of Will. In Chapter 6 ("The Monster"), he and Joyce visit Ives' home to learn more. Her sister Becky lets them in, but Terry, they discover, is now catatonic.

Becky fills in a number of gaps: the CIA-sanctioned research program, Project MKUltra, she says, preyed on susceptible people like her sister, promising them a couple hundred dollars to participate in psychedelic drug tests and other mind-bending experiments. Those tests, it turned out, were far more involved and dangerous than advertised. Terry, Becky reveals, was often stripped naked and put in isolation tanks, where they would attempt to test the limits of consciousness.

We also learn that Terry was pregnant at the time. Becky, and the general public, believe she miscarried in the third trimester. But we later learn via flashback that baby Jane (Eleven) was indeed delivered in Hawkins Laboratory and taken from her mother. After her lawsuit failed, Terry attempted to take things into her own hands and rescue her daughter from the facility at gunpoint. However, after finding her daughter in the "Rainbow Room" she was apprehended, tied down, and subjected to electroshock therapy, permanently scrambling her brain and leaving her in a vegetative state.

How grounded is any of this in actual history? Project MKUltra was indeed the code name for a real CIA program begun in the early 1950s. Its purpose was to develop drugs and techniques that might be used for interrogations and the manipulation of Soviet enemies. Thousands of American human subjects were used in these experiments, which included a range of mind-altering drugs, including LSD, and a number of mind-control techniques, including hypnosis, sensory deprivation, and psychological torture. Most of these covert activities, of course, were illegal, and conducted, like Hawkins Lab, at institutions purporting to be something else.

The program was in peak operation from 1953 to 1964, and officially dissolved in the mid-1970s, though rumors persisted that it continued to operate clandestinely. In 1977, a Freedom of Information Act request unveiled 20,000 documents related to Project MKUltra, though many more were destroyed.

The Duffer Brothers acknowledge being fascinated by such secret programs. Said Ross Duffer: "Whether it was MKUltra or the Philadelphia Experiment where the government—true or not—was doing stuff where it was trying to put the boundaries of science in this sort of race with the Cold War. To us, it was the idea of, 'What if they're pushing a little bit too far here?' And, of course, there are conspiracy theories out there where [people] say that they did. It was more believable than that in some small town—that this would happen in this race with Russia."

This Is Our Government

Beyond such controversial conspiracies, Hawkins National Laboratory oversees an elaborate surveillance program. It seems to have ears and eyes everywhere. Phone conversations are listened in on; houses are bugged; patient exams are video recorded. Lab agents invade the homes of both the Byers and Wheelers, taking photos and seizing possessions. Nancy and Jonathan, of course, are closely monitored once they begin seeking the truth. In Season 2, Chapter 4 ("Will the Wise") they are stalked and spied on at a park, resulting in their temporary apprehension and custody inside Hawkins Lab. Chapter 6 is actually called "The Spy" (a reference, in this case, to Will and the Mind Flayer). But surveillance, in various forms, is ubiquitous in the series. Such intrusive activities, again, are not far removed from American history.

In his Inaugural Address in 1981, Ronald Reagan famously declared that "government is not the solution to our problem; government is the problem." Reagan promised to shrink Big Government—to get bloated budgets, bureaucratic tape, and burdensome taxes out of the way of ordinary people. While he did indeed reduce taxes and slash many social programs, however, the government continued to grow in size and reach. Federal spending nearly doubled during the Reagan era, as did the national debt. A substantial chunk of this spending was Cold War-related—that is, it was used in an effort to stay ahead of the Soviet Union through enormous investments in the military, intelligence-gathering, and national defense.

Most people are at least somewhat familiar with the US Patriot Act of 2001, but long before George W. Bush's controversial surveillance act was signed into law, there was Ronald Reagan's Executive Order 12333. Executive Order 12333 gave US intelligence agencies unprecedented power to spy on and collect information from U.S. citizens. The law did not require that a citizen be suspected of wrongdoing and placed no restrictions on what communications could be collected and retained. It raised serious questions, that is, about privacy and civil liberties that seemed to directly contradict the notion of an unobtrusive government. (Such questions remain relevant today, not only with the federal government, but also with corporate tech giants like Facebook and Google, whose far-reaching data collecting practices have come under fire.)

For many American citizens in the '80s, including those who claimed to be for small government, such principles were often compromised in the name of patriotism. When federal agents from Hawkins Lab descend on the Wheeler house in Season 1, Chapter 7 ("The Bathtub"), for example, scouring the premises and carting away boxes of possessions, the Wheelers ultimately accept it as necessary. Dr. Brenner, in essence, asks for their blind trust and cooperation and they consent. "This is our government," Ted Wheeler reasons. "They're on our side."

Of course, not everyone is as cooperative. We first meet Murray Bauman (played by Brett Gelman) at the beginning of Season 2. A former investigative reporter for the *Chicago Sun-Times,* he now resides in a fortress-like bunker in Sesser, Illinois. In Season 2, Chapter 1 ("MADMAX"), he makes a trip to the Hawkins Police Department to talk to Chief Hopper about a potential "Russian spy presence" in town. From the response to his assertion, we get the sense that Bauman is perceived locally as a nutty, paranoid, conspiracy theorist. Yet as novelist Joseph Heller put it: "just because you're paranoid doesn't mean they aren't after you."

Murray Bauman has been hired as a private investigator by Barb's parents to dig deeper into their daughter's disappearance. His investigation eventually intersects with that of Nancy and Jonathan, who show up at his house in Season 2, Chapter 5 ("Dig Dug").

Prior to meeting with Bauman, Nancy and Jonathan managed to make their way into the belly of the beast—Hawkins National Laboratory—where, after being held against their will, they are given a mini-tour of the premises by Dr. Owens—and an explanation for Barb's death. Mistakes have been made, he acknowledges. But the men responsible for those mistakes, including Dr. Brenner, are gone. The Lab's job now, he explains, is to contain and harness the monster (literal and figurative) that Brenner unleashed.

Dr. Owens takes them to the command center, where they see for themselves the ominous portal that leads to the Upside Down. Its rapid growth, Dr. Owens explains, requires constant vigilance and secrecy. "You see why I have to stop the truth from spreading, too, just the same as those weeds there — by any means necessary." Not only is it dangerous to the town of Hawkins, Dr. Owens explains, but it could potentially fall into the wrong hands. "Imagine for a moment if a foreign state, let's say the Soviets, heard about our mistake. You think they would even consider it a mistake. What if they tried to replicate it?"

Dr. Owens seems to assume a couple of teenagers will be content with his rationale. After they leave, however, we learn that Nancy recorded the conversation on her Walkman. Unlike her father, she is not placated by patriotic duty; she wants justice and accountability. "Let's burn that lab to the ground," she declares to Jonathan.

Behind the Curtain

With tape in hand, Nancy and Jonathan drive straight to Murray Bauman's house in Illinois. After allowing them into his private complex, Bauman—clad in bathrobe—leads them to his own command center, which is populated with notes, pictures, clippings, and potential leads. As intricate as his timeline and theory is, Nancy and Jonathan help clarify, correct, and fill gaps. They play him the tape from Hawkins lab. "Is it incriminating?" asks Nancy. It is, says Bauman. But nobody will believe it. "Those people," he says, "They're not wired like me and you, okay? They don't spend their lives trying to get a look at what's behind the curtain. They like the curtain. It provides them stability, comfort, definition."

All it will take to discredit the tape, he tells Nancy and Jonathan, is someone with authority telling the public it is fake. That's how power works. Those in authority create the terms of reality and everyone else—or most everyone—goes along. The only hope, he eventually concludes (with the help of some vodka), is to dilute the truth. Water it down. Make the story less elaborate, "more tolerable." Say that Barb was exposed to toxins, and that the Lab tried to cover it up, rather than that they were conducting illegal experiments on human subjects (including children) in a misguided attempt to beat the Soviets and accidentally unleashed a monster from an alternate dimension.

In this way, Murray proves more savvy—and self-aware—than your run-of-the-mill conspiracy theorist. His plan ultimately succeeds. In Season 2, Chapter 9 ("The Gate"), we see Hawkins National Laboratory closed down, as military vehicles file out. Murray Bauman sits in a lawn chair, waving, as a news report narrates that the US Department of Energy acknowledged wrongdoing in the death and cover-up of Barbara Holland.

Such acts of vigilance and courageous persistence of the truth—by Nancy, Jonathan, Murray, and many others—the show suggests, are the truly patriotic acts. As are the acts of genuine humanity and creative resistance by the kids.

Some critics have noted that movies from the Reagan era rather consistently cast the United States government in negative light—a vast, secretive, overreaching entity that doesn't always act in the interest of its own citizens. Journalist David Sirota describes Spielberg's *E.T.*, for example, as an "anti-government parable about children having to flee faceless, jackbooted federal agents." One might make a similar case against *Stranger Things*.

Yet *Stranger Things* is not so much anti-government as it is pro-government accountability. It highlights the reality that unchecked power and secrecy often leads to bad outcomes—as the actual Project MKUltra experiments and invasive surveillance efforts, among numerous other examples, demonstrate.

In the final chapter of Season 2 ("The Gate"), Chief Hopper finds a wounded Dr. Owens bleeding to death in a stairwell in Hawkins Lab. He helps stop the bleeding, but also asks him to consider an appeal. Since Eleven is about to save everyone, he suggests, maybe Hawkins Lab can finally do right by her. "Maybe you can help her lead a normal life," he says, "one where she's not poked and prodded, and treated like a lab rat."

Dr. Owens ultimately honors this request, obtaining a birth certificate for Eleven in which she is no longer a number, or a test subject, or a weapon, but a human being: Jane Hopper.

This act obviously doesn't absolve Hawkins Lab from its abuses and crimes. But it does show that there are individuals, even within a system riddled with corruption, willing to push back against power and do.

7

Playing Games

In Season 2, Chapter 9 ("The Gate"), Steve tries to use a sports analogy to drive home a point. "If Coach calls a play," he says, "bottom line, you execute it." The kids look at him like he's an alien. It's the wrong audience. "Okay, first of all," responds Mike, "this isn't some stupid sports game. Second of all, we're not even in the game; we're on the bench." The exchange is indicative of the minimal role sports plays in the series. Those just aren't the games these kids are into.

Other than Steve and Billy's basketball showdown in Chapter 3—which Joe Keery (Steve Harrington) describes as having a "homoerotic...*Top Gun* volleyball sort of [vibe]" —we never really see or even hear about sports in the series. There are no Friday night lights, no posters of '80s basketball stars Magic Johnson or Indiana native Larry Bird in bedrooms. There is no mention of the Bobby Knight-led Indiana Hoosiers, a powerhouse in the '80s that won national championships in 1981 and 1987. These kids simply aren't into sports. They are, as Lucas's sister Erica memorably puts it, a "bunch o' nerds."

D&D

What the boys in *Stranger Things* are into is Dungeons & Dragons, a game that does not simply make a one-time cameo as in *E.T.*, but is artfully woven into the language and framework of the story.

The fantasy role-playing game first came out in 1974, the brainchild of Gary Gygax and Dave Arneson. It grew in popularity in the late 70s and '80s, establishing a subculture of enthusiasts drawn to its emphasis on intelligence, camaraderie, and imagination. Before long, multiple books were published elaborating on its intricate rules and concepts. By 1981, D&D had an estimated three million players and was widely associated with geek culture. The game is credited not only with bridging the worlds of fantasy and gaming, but also for establishing a successful blueprint for role-playing games.

Tactical Studies Rules, Inc. (TSR), which published the game, created two distinct iterations after its initial wave of popularity: the first was more simplified and accessible, aimed at the general public; the second, referred to as Advanced Dungeons & Dragons (AD&D) was for more serious players and required greater knowledge and fluency.

As we see at the beginning of Season 1, Chapter 1 ("The Vanishing of Will Byers") in *Stranger Things*, D&D is typically played around a table with a board, polyhedral dice, and miniature figurines. Those figurines represent specific characters with specific specialties. So, for example, in the kids' game in the Wheeler basement, Mike plays the Dungeon Master (the game's referee/storyteller), Lucas plays a knight, Dustin plays a dwarf, and Will plays a wizard.

The group as a whole is referred to as a "Party." Each character plays an important role in the overall "campaign," while also developing individual attributes and powers. A campaign can go on for hours, even days, as the Party problem-solves, battles, gathers knowledge, and embarks on various adventures. In *Stranger Things,* we learn that the game the boys are playing at the beginning of Chapter 1 took weeks of planning and was going on for about ten hours before Mrs. Wheeler called it off.

It is easy to see D&D's appeal to Mike, Will, Dustin and Lucas, four boys with active imaginations and a love of adventure; it is also not hard to see how it operates as a metaphor for their real-life exploits and foreshadows events to come. For example, in that opening scene in Chapter 1, Will is forced to face down the Demogorgon. Lucas advises him to "fireball" it, while Dustin tells him to cast a protection spell. Will decides to fireball, but rolls a seven (he needed a thirteen or higher), meaning he was defeated by the Demogorgon. Not long after finishing the game, of course, Will is chased down and snatched from his shed by a mysterious monster the boys refer to as the Demogorgon.

Such connections between the game and real life, particularly in assigning names to things outside of ordinary experiences, recur throughout the series. "These kids were big D&D nerds," explains Matt Duffer, "so they can understand this through the Dungeons & Dragons mythology and terminology. And that makes everything that's happening easier to understand for the kids than it does for the adults. They have been introduced to these concepts before. And then of course they have their Mr. Clarke, their 1980's Wikipedia. So it's fun and it's challenging for the characters to figure out what's going on. They have to use what's at their disposal, which is Dungeons & Dragons and their science teacher." Numerous terms used in the show, thus, originate from Dungeons & Dragons, although they are not so much exact correlations as approximations.

So, what is a Demogorgon? In D&D, it represents the "Prince of Demons," a very rare creature that struck fear in players of the game, possessing a Voldemort-like mystique. In the D&D *Monster Manual* its stat block reveals devastating powers and protections. We see it represented in the game as a dual-headed, lizard-like creature. Confronting it in the context of D&D meant near-certain death.

Such demonic characters led to what the BBC describes as "the great 1980s Dungeons & Dragons panic." Gradually, as the game increased in popularity, some parents became concerned about its influence on young minds, particularly after two teenage fans of the game committed suicide (there was no evidence that D&D was responsible for their deaths). Conservative Christian groups denounced it as "an occult tool that opens up young people to influence or possession by demons." Concerned parents, meanwhile, launched the action group Bothered About Dungeons and Dragons (BADD) in 1983, blaming the game for encouraging Satanism, sex perversion, and suicide, among other things.

While the controversy eventually waned, it speaks to how unfamiliar role-playing games were at the time, and how subversive its emphasis on fantasy and the supernatural was in more traditional homes.

For the characters in *Stranger Things*, however, it offers a useful framework to explain and articulate their real-life encounters and adventures. In Chapter 5 ("The Flea and the Acrobat"), for example, Eleven flips the D&D board upside down to illustrate that Will is hiding in another dimension. "Like the Vale of Shadows!" exclaims Dustin. The kids look the term up in a well-worn copy of the *D&D Expert Rulebook* (the 1983 edition). "The Vale of Shadows is a dimension that is a dark reflection, or echo, of our world," it reads. "It is a place of decay and death, a plane out of phase, a [place] with monsters. It is right next to you and you don't even see it." Likewise, Eleven uses the Demogorgon figurine to explain that there is an actual monster in the Upside Down that poses a threat to Will, and others.

When Will is finally rescued in Season 1, Chapter 8 ("The Upside Down"), we once again see the boys gathered together around a D&D board in the Wheeler basement. And once again, the events in the game resemble what transpires in real life. This time the story revolves around a lost knight, a proud princess, and weird flowers in a cave. While interpretations vary among fans of the show, the internet developed something of a consensus around the knight being Chief Hopper, the princess being Eleven, and the weird flowers being the Demogorgon eggs or vines that begin to spread underground in Season 2. The fearsome Thessalhydra, meanwhile, might represent the Mind Flayer, which Will triumphs over in the game (and later, with help from his friends, in real life).

What is the Mind Flayer? When Will first sees it in the early chapters of Season 2 he calls it the Shadow Monster. The term Mind Flayer is introduced by Dustin in Chapter 8 ("The Mind Flayer"). Dustin not only seems to have an encyclopedic knowledge of D&D; he also loves giving things names (see also: demodogs and D'Artagnan). As Mike explains the characteristics of the Shadow Monster —the hive mind, the brain, the desire to control—Dustin once again thinks in D&D terms. "Like the Mind Flayer," he says. They look the term up in Will's *D&D Expert Rulebook* and immediately see the connections. It has tentacles; it is highly evil; and, as Dustin explains, "It enslaves races of other dimensions by taking over their brains using its highly-developed psionic powers."

As with all of the D&D terms used in the show, the parallels are not intended to be exact. In D&D, for example, the Mind Flayer is a humanoid that only resides in subterranean places. The Mind Flayer in *Stranger Things*, by contrast, is an enormous spider-like creature towering in the sky. The Duffer Brothers drew from a range of inspirations for its form and characteristics, including the work of H. P. Lovecraft. Then they went looking through a D&D manual to see if they could find something similar. That's when they found the Mind Flayer. "It has nothing to do with the shape, or the way it looks, or the particles," explains Ross Duffer. "But the fact that it moves from dimension to dimension, infecting the minds of others in order to control them and spread itself. I can't remember everything else, but it's everything that we were talking about with our Shadow Monster."

In Season 2, the boys also get new D&D-based character roles. When newcomer Max asks to join the Party, Mike declares that all the roles are filled: he is the Paladin (the holy knight/leader), Lucas is the Ranger (the warrior and hunter), Dustin is the Bard (well-versed in spells and language), and Eleven is the Mage (the Wizard with special psionic powers). Max suggests that she could be the Zoomer, but that suggestion is rejected. It appears that Mike sees her as a threat to the group's cohesion and focus, similar to how Lucas felt about Eleven in Season 1.

There are a couple of other significant references to D&D in Season 2. Among Will's drawings and self-portraits we see one in which he is "Will, the Wise" (Chapter 4, in fact, is called "Will the Wise"). In this role, he is not a victim or freak or zombie, but a wizard-like character, valiantly leading a group into battle. Mike also believes Will has "truesight," a D&D term that indicates the ability to see invisible creatures and objects, detect illusions, and penetrate alternate dimensions. Perhaps, Mike reasons, Will's episodes aren't flashbacks; perhaps they are real visions into the Upside Down.

Just as The Clash's "Should I Stay or Should I Go" was not merely used as soundtrack but interwoven into the characters and storyline, so, similarly, Dungeons & Dragons is far more than a prop or nostalgic game reference; it offers a symbolic mythology through which the characters—and audience—navigate through their adventures.

Video Games

While Dungeons & Dragons plays a crucial role in the first two seasons of *Stranger Things*, it is not the only game we see integrated into the show. The 1980s also saw the birth of video games and the explosion of arcades. "We were hoping to do with the arcade [in season 2] what we did in season one with D&D," explains Ross Duffer, "which was to do a bit of foreshadowing for the whole season, with Lucas getting Princess Daphne, and the monsters in Dig-Dug. We were hoping to roughly set up where we were going to go in the next nine hours."

In addition to providing a narrative frame, it also hearkens back to a brief moment in American history—roughly 1978-1983—when arcades were *the* Holy Temple of Recreation for kids and teenagers. They remained popular for another decade, but the early '80s represents the peak. A 1982 cover story for *Time* declared that video games were "blitzing the world," estimating that arcades in America had increased to over 13,000.

New, groundbreaking games seemed to appear every week. First came games like *Space Invaders* and *Asteroids,* both of which could be found in just about every arcade in the late 70s/early '80s. Then, in 1980, came *Pac-Man*, which became the most successful video game of its era and a social phenomenon. Hundreds of thousands of machines were sold in its first year alone. Those machines generated an astounding 1 billion dollars in quarters in a single year—higher gross revenues than *Star Wars*. *Pac-Man* was also credited for bringing in more girls (an estimated 60% of its players were female, far more than any other game at the time).

Pac-Man became the most iconic game of the early video game industry, but there were plenty of others that captured young people's imaginations, including games like *Centipede*, *Frogger*, *Galaga*, *Donkey Kong*, and *Tron*. The latter game was a tie-in to the futuristic 1982 movie of the same name. When it first hit arcades, the fluorescent blue and black machine was often set aside in a featured area, where one might wait hours to have their turn to take control of the glowing blue joystick.

It is difficult to convey the sense of wonder and excitement arcades created in their early years. It was a much different experience than gaming today: for one, most everyone was standing up, but more significantly, it was a social, communal experience. Going to the arcade was like entering some action-packed, quarter-clanking, neon wonderland. You'd meet your friends there. You'd play amazing new games. You'd eat junk food. You'd check out the girl or boy you liked. And for the most part, parents were nowhere to be seen.

Like *Dungeons & Dragons*, arcades generated controversy. Some people believed they were rotting children's brains; others, meanwhile, saw them as a hedonistic dens for illicit behavior; still others worried it was an easy target for predators and kidnappers. Yet for the most part, such dangers were overhyped. For those who came of age during this period, this iteration of the arcade—not the current, stale Chuck E Cheese or Dave & Busters model—brings back warm memories. As photography editor Rian Dundon writes: "the jingling quarters, sticky plastic surfaces and crunchy carpeting of the arcade will always conjure deviant yearnings for those glowy-dark sanctuaries our mothers always warned us about."

Stranger Things allows us to re-enter one of these sanctuaries at the beginning of Season 2, Chapter 1 (MADMAX). Before they arrive at the arcade, we see the kids scrounging for quarters—well, Dustin is scrounging; Lucas has been working "like a man" to earn some extra coin; Mike, meanwhile, decides to steal change out of his sister Nancy's piggy bank. They arrive on their bikes (except Will, who is dropped off by his mom due to his abduction the prior year). As expected, we see lots of kids and teenagers in and around the arcade. In fact, the only supervising we see is from the perfectly cast, cheeto-chomping, acne-ridden teenage employee, Keith.

The *Stranger Things* production crew went to great lengths to re-create an authentic-looking and feeling arcade. Recalls Ross Duffer: "Our production designer took this abandoned space — it was just incredible — and completely turned it into the Palace. For us, just as video-game nerds, it was really a dream come true." They named it the Palace after the arcade in *WarGames*, the 1983 cold war science fiction cult classic, and packed it with real, functioning arcade machines.

The first game the kids play is *Dragon's Lair*. Released in 1983, *Dragon's Lair* was the first major LaserDisc game to hit the market in the U.S. This meant that unlike a traditional video game like *Asteroids* or *Pac-Man*, it used pre-recorded animated graphics—created, for this game, by the legendary Don Bluth (known for such animated films as *The Secret of Nimh*, *An American Tail*, and *The Land Before Time*). In a way, it was like being integrated into a cartoon or animated film.

Dragon's Lair was enormously popular and inspired a number of other LaserDisc video games. In fact, the Duffers remember playing it as kids. However, it was also often criticized for a number of problems and glitches, including commonly going black as graphics switched. It was also one of the most difficult games to win and required two quarters to play (note that Dustin refers to it as an "overpriced piece of shit").

The basic storyline of *Dragon's Lair* is simple and familiar: Dirk the Knight must clear a number of obstacles to rescue Princess Daphne, who, as we see in *Stranger Things*, is a hypersexualized damsel in distress, no doubt intended for adolescents. In addition to such titillation and its cutting edge effects, however, the boys in *Stranger Things* are also likely attracted to it because of its emphasis on being fully immersed into a story—more specifically, a quest. In this way, it is similar to Dungeons & Dragons, beckoning the boys to be heroes by undertaking a challenging adventure.

We see a number of other popular early-'80s games around the arcade: *Pac-Man, Ms. Pac-Man, Galaga, Missile Command,* and *Pole Position,* among others. The other big one we see the kids drawn to besides *Dragon's Lair,* though, is *Dig Dug.* Released in 1982, *Dig Dug* was ranked #6 in a list of Top Coin-operated Video Games of All Time. Like Pac-Man, its maze-like structure and simple concept made it accessible and addictive. Dustin proudly maintains the high score on the machine until he is informed by Keith that he has been superseded. The boys rush over to the machine to find that someone named "MADMAX" now has the high score of 751,300. This, of course, leads to their discovery and fascination with the new girl in town: Max.

The objective of *Dig Dug* is to eliminate underground monsters. In this way, the game was clearly not a random choice on the part of the Duffers, as it effectively foreshadows the underground terrain in which much of Season 2 takes place (Chapter 5, in fact, is titled "Dig Dug"), as well as the mission they embark on (ie killing the monsters—demodogs—that lurk there). As with so many other things in *Stranger Things,* the line between the fantasy-game world and real life is effectively blurred.

Puzzles

We see a handful of other games in *Stranger Things.* Puzzles appear sporadically throughout the series, especially in Season 2. When Bob comes to check on Joyce and Will in Season 2, Chapter 4

("Will the Wise"), he brings a pile of logic games and brain teasers, including Hi-Q Hexed and Soma Cube. It is their presence, and Bob's reminder of his nickname ("Bob the Brain"), in fact, that prompts Joyce to ask him for help solving the biggest puzzle of Season 2: the meaning of Will's elaborate drawings.

This seems to be the overriding message of *Stranger Things* when it comes to games: they are important—for the imagination, for the intellect, for bonding and collaborating. In the '80s, new games— including D&D and video games—elicited concerns among many parents. Video games and arcades, in particular, became the subject of endless debate and discussion. As historian Michael Newman writes:

> The popularity of video games in the '80s prompted educators, psychotherapists, local government officeholders and media commentators to warn that young players were likely to suffer serious negative effects. The games would influence their aficionados in the all the wrong ways. They would harm children's eyes and might cause "Space Invaders Wrist" and other physical ailments. Like television, they would be addictive, like a drug. Games would inculcate violence and aggression in impressionable youngsters. Their players would do poorly in school and become isolated and desensitized. A reader wrote to *The New York Times* to complain that video games were "cultivating a generation of mindless, ill-tempered adolescents.

Yet for all the panic and controversy surrounding these games, the generation that came of age on them managed to survive. Indeed, some discovered that they could be useful, even educational for young people. As the kids in *Stranger Things* find out: Who knows when you might need to problem-solve, figure out a new concept, or embark on a perilous quest?

While they may not have saved Princess Daphne in *Dragon's Lair*, they did manage to navigate treacherous tunnels crawling with monsters and save Will (and Hawkins)—at least for the time-being—from the Mind Flayer. And just like at the arcade, Lucas gets the girl.

8

———

Science & Technology

In *Stranger Things*, the Hawkins AV Club is the perfect distillation of the show's love affair with science and technology. It serves as both nerd sanctuary and ideas hub. It is the designated meeting place at school for Mike, Will, Dustin, and Lucas (and later Eleven and Max), whether for brainstorming sessions or crises. It is where they huddle together when Will goes missing, as well as when Dustin discovers his mysterious pet, D'Artagnan.

The first time we see the kids in their AV Club element is in Season 1, Chapter 1 ("The Vanishing of Will Byers"). While most of the students in Mr. Clarke's class are eager to leave, the boys stay after, eagerly anticipating the arrival of a new technological device: a Heathkit ham shack.

Heathkit was still a prominent producer of kits and electronic products in the 1980s, many of which were made for educational purposes. Mr. Clarke allows the kids to sit down and try out the new radio transmitter (which seems to be a DX-60 Amateur Transmitter). "I bet you could talk to New York on this thing!" exclaims Dustin. "Think bigger," responds Mr. Clarke. Turns out, it can reach Australia, a revelation that immediately has the kids trying out their best Australian accents.

For a few decades, AV Clubs—the AV stands for audiovisual—flourished in American schools. New technology was exciting for kids and the AV Club gave them a chance to learn about and use everything from transistor radios to video cameras. The Hawkins AV room is pretty typical of what spaces often looked like in the '80s: a closet-like room overflowing with speakers, amplifiers, cameras, televisions, stereos, headphones, and tapes. Depending on the school budget and supervisor, some AV rooms, of course, were more barren and dusty. But at Hawkins Middle School, Mr. Clarke has clearly created an active, stimulating environment.

In Season 2, we even see an Apple poster, with the original rainbow-scheme icon, hanging on the wall in the AV Club room. Since Season 2 takes place in 1984, it would have been the same year Apple ran its famous Ridley Scott-directed "1984" commercial during the Super Bowl announcing the arrival of the game-changing Apple Macintosh personal computer (later rebranded as the Macintosh 128K). While we don't see one of those computers in the room yet, it seems likely Mr. Clarke will try to get funding for it before long.

The small, dark, technology-cluttered AV room is featured in numerous episodes. In Season 1, Chapter 4 ("The Body"), the boys decide to take Eleven to school to see if the Heathkit will allow a stronger connection to reach Will. As soon as they arrive, they make a b-line to the AV Club Room; however, it is locked. Mr. Clarke finds them loitering by the door and promises if they attend the assembly for Will, the Heathkit will be theirs for the rest of the day, tossing Mike the keys.

After the assembly, they rush back to the AV room and Mike gets the device set up, as El sits down in the dark room and closes her eyes. Initially it triggers a flashback. But before long, they hear their lost friend, desperately calling out for help. "It's like home," he cries out, "but it's so dark...so dark and empty and cold..." The connection is so strong the machine suddenly bursts into flames, setting off the fire alarm. Dustin, however, alertly locates a fire extinguisher and puts the fire out before it spreads further. While the heathkit doesn't allow them to save Will, then, it does show their impulse to turn to science and technology—mixed with a healthy dose of imagination—to solve problems.

The AV Room is also where Dustin organizes an impromptu meeting in Season 2, Chapter 3 ("The Pollywog"), to reveal his new discovery: the unusual, pollywog-like creature he has named D'Artagnan (Dart for short). Dustin passes the creature around, before launching into a research debriefing. Dart doesn't seem to be an amphibian or reptile. This leads Dustin to believe he may have discovered a new species (a discovery that he is adamant no one, including Mr. Clarke, steal from him).

Before Dustin is able to share the creature with Mr. Clarke, however, Mike orders an urgent AV Club meeting. That cute creature, he warns, might be from the Upside Down. A vigorous debate ensues, before they decide to look at the creature again. Sure enough, it has grown dramatically and sprouts legs right before their eyes. Mike attempts to squash it with the Heathkit microphone, but it eludes him. Max, meanwhile, who has been left out of the meeting, finally manages to pick the lock to the room, allowing Dart to scurry out the door and down the hall.

Once again, this scene demonstrates the kids' curiosity and proclivity to turn to science for answers. Dustin does an impressive amount of research before determining he may have made a major discovery. But it is the AV Club Room that offers a safe space at school, untethered by routine or regimentation, for the kids to discuss, debate, explore, and learn.

Bob the Brain

How does a small town in Indiana have such a cutting-edge AV Club? In Season 2, Chapter 8 ("The Mind Flayer"), we learn that it might not have existed in Hawkins at all if not for the passion and initiative of a beloved *Stranger Things* character: Bob Newby. Bob, Mike reveals, was the original founder of the Hawkins AV Club. He petitioned the school for its existence and held a fundraiser to buy equipment.

Bob's love of technology is obvious throughout Season 2. We learn, for example, that he is the manager of the local RadioShack. In the 1980s, RadioShack was *the* destination store for techies (the company branded themselves, appropriately, as "The technology store," because there simply wasn't anyone else in the same league). Its catalogs were legendary—long before Amazon or Best Buy, it seemed to brim with endless new gadgets and electronics, from remote control cars to calculator watches to Sony Walkmans. The year we see Bob working there—1984—in fact, marked the premiere of the first mobile phone. Unlike the empty ghost stores they ultimately became (Radio Shack filed bankruptcy in 2015), retail outlets in malls and downtowns buzzed with enthusiasm.

When we first see Bob at RadioShack in Season 2, Chapter 3 ("The Pollywog"), he is fiddling away on some wires with nose-pliers in the Service and Repairs department. Joyce calls to ask about a tape from Halloween: it's too small to fit in the VCR, she says. Bob launches into a jargon-filled explanation that sounds like a foreign language to Joyce. So he tries again in simpler terms, directing her to plug the coaxial cables into the back of the TV as well as in the camcorder. Easy peasy. It works!

Joyce watches the footage of Bob on Halloween night, dressed as Dracula, explaining to Will how to operate the camcorder, including how to zoom in and out. That classic black and red camcorder—the JVC GR-C1—was released in 1984 and became an instant hit as the first all-in-one VHS camcorder. Incidentally, the exact same model was used by Marty McFly and Doc Brown in *Back to the Future*. Its original retail was over $1,000, though perhaps Bob got some kind of discount as manager of RadioShack. In any case, given its hefty price tag, it is incredibly generous of him to entrust the camcorder to Will for trick or treating.

The footage Will recorded that night also alerts Joyce to a statticky visual that resembles Will's drawings of the Shadow Monster. As Matt Duffer explains, "There was interference. This creature and this other world, it affects the electromagnetic field. That's what caused all the Christmas lights to flicker last year. So it's taking that idea and expanding on it. We like the idea that this video camera was able to, in a way, capture a burn-in or a photograph of this thing that had affected this camera."

Bob's tech knowledge is later put to use in Hawkins Laboratory. With the building on lockdown and swarming with demodogs, the remaining group's only hope of getting out is to reset the breakers. As one might expect, Chief Hopper volunteers first. But Bob explains that the job is not as simple as simply flipping the breakers. Since the locks are fail-secure, once the power comes back on, someone needs to completely reboot the computer system and override the security codes with manual input. "How do I do that?" asks Hopper. "You can't," responds Bob, "Not unless you know BASIC."

BASIC, as Mike clarifies, refers to a computer programming language. That language was invented in the 1960s, and was commonly used in microcomputers in the 1980s, allowing individuals and businesses to develop custom software for some of the very purposes we see in Hawkins Lab. Bob is the only one in the building that knows the language. As that dawns on him, he realizes he is the one that must descend three flights of stairs in a pitch-black building crawling with ravenous demodogs. "I got this," he says, taking a deep breath. Then he turns to Joyce: "Remember, Bob Newby: superhero."

In his final act, Bob showcases his tech savvy and executes his mission to perfection. With a flashlight and gun in hand, he makes his way down the hall and stairs, which are littered with dead bodies. Then he locates the breakers and switches them on, before sitting down at the green-lettered IBM computer, rapidly typing in code to unlock the doors. Bob, of course, doesn't ultimately make it out alive. But his computer acumen saves everyone else. Tech superhero, indeed.

Lessons From Mr. Clarke

In addition to founding the AV Club and saving the group from Hawkins Lab, we also learn that Bob Newby mentored another science and tech guru in the the show: Mr. Scott Clarke. A science teacher at Hawkins Middle School, Mr. Clarke is the kind of educator who goes above and beyond classroom duties—especially for those few students who seem genuinely curious and eager to learn. The Duffer Brothers describe him as the boys' personal Wikipedia.

When the boys find themselves stuck solving a problem, he is the one they frequently turn to. In Season 1, Chapter Five ("The Flea and the Acrobat"), for example, they seek him out after Will's funeral—not, as one might expect, to ask what happens when one dies, but to better understand the nature of inter-dimensional travel.

"So you know how in *Cosmos*, Carl Sagan talks about other dimensions, like beyond our world?" Mike asks. Mr. Clarke says that, yes, in theory, that is right. It is yet another spot-on '80s reference. *Cosmos* was a groundbreaking TV series narrated by renowned cosmologist Carl Sagan about the origins of life and our place in the universe. Premiering in 1980 on PBS, it was the most watched documentary series in American history to that point. It asked big questions and evoked a sense of wonder and lyrical sweep to our cosmic journey. *The New York Times* described it as "a watershed moment for science-themed television programming." It makes sense then that inquisitive kids like Mike, Dustin, and Lucas would have watched it.

As always, Mr. Clarke doesn't talk down to the kids. In fact, he pulls out his own science reference: American physicist Hugh Everett's "many-worlds interpretation," which asserts that all possible pasts and futures are real, each existing in its own world, or dimension. "Basically," explains Mr. Clarke, "there are parallel universes—just like our world, but infinite variations of it." So, in theory, every possible path of life plays out in one dimension or another.

Mr. Clarke assumes they are asking such questions to seek solace about Will's death. But really, they explain, their inquiries are more pragmatic: they want to know how one might actually travel to a different dimension. To answer this, Mr. Clarke uses an analogy (that also serves as the title of the episode): the flea and the acrobat. On a paper plate he draws an acrobat on a tightrope, which represents our dimension. In this dimension he can move forward or backward. But the flea can move on the side of the rope, or even the bottom. A light bulb clicks on for the boys. "The Upside Down," they say in unison.

But how do they get there if they are the acrobat, asks Dustin. Mr. Clarke explains that it would take a massive amount of energy, more than we are currently capable of, plus some kind of tear in the space-time continuum. To illustrate, Mr. Clarke bends the plate in half and punches a hole through it. The hole represents the doorway or portal to another dimension. Even still, if such a tear existed, Mr. Clarke says, it might disrupt gravity, electromagnetic fields, and potentially swallow us up whole. "Science is neat," he says, "but I'm afraid it's not very forgiving."

Far from discouraging the boys, though, Mr. Clarke's lesson helps them to understand the reality of other dimensions, and inspires them to use their compasses to find the portal to the Upside Down.

The boys learn a number of other science lessons from Mr. Clarke. In Season 1, Chapter 7 ("The Bathtub"), Dustin calls him at home about a "science question"—specifically, how to build a sensory deprivation tank. Since it is a Saturday night, and he is on a date, Mr. Clarke suggests they pick up the question on Monday after school. But Dustin persists, reminding Mr. Clarke that he urged them to never stop being curious. "Why are you keeping this curiosity door locked?" he asks in characteristically Dustin fashion. Mr. Clarke relinquishes, providing Dustin instructions on how to build such a tank over the phone.

The lessons continue in Season 2. In Chapter 1 ("MADMAX"), we see Mr. Clarke teaching the class about the human brain (while also welcoming newcomer Max on the "curiosity voyage"). In Chapter 3 ("The Pollywog"), he delivers a lesson about the curious case of Phineas Gage, an American railroad construction foreman who survived an accident in which an iron rod was driven through his skull. While his survival was miraculous, it changed his personality, eliciting endless fascination and inquiry about why and how.

In Chapter 4 ("Will the Wise"), Mr. Clarke gives a lesson on our fight or flight instinct. All living things, he says, respond to danger in similar ways. "We're very much the same when we encounter danger," he says in an almost Rod Serling-like narration, "our hearts start pounding, our palms start to sweat. These are the signs of the physical and emotional state we call fear." Such lessons are not only instructive; they act as a subtext to the events that are unfolding in the show.

Into the Future

The presence of Mr. Clarke in *Stranger Things* is indicative of a broader renaissance of enthusiasm for science in the 1980s. While the Reagan Administration slashed the National Science Foundation by 70%, science education found ways to flourish, including popular new TV shows for kids like *3-2-1 Contact*, which aired on PBS from 1980 to 1988 and was used often in classrooms. *Cosmos*, likewise, was used in classrooms and Carl Sagan became a cultural icon—perhaps the biggest scientific celebrity since Albert Einstein. His charisma and passion was infectious, turning an entire generation on to the wonders and mysteries of universe.

The '80s also saw the emergence of theoretical physicist Stephen Hawking, whose classic book, *A Brief History of Time* (which included an introduction by Sagan), became an unexpected sensation in 1988. That book, which spent an astounding 100 weeks on the bestseller list, catapulted Stephen Hawking into a celebrity in his own right. Paralyzed by a slow-progressing motor neurone disease, Hawking learned to communicate through a computer-generated speech synthesizer. That techno-logically mediated voice became recognized throughout the world, giving Hawking an almost oracle-like mystique and symbolizing the power of science and technology to overcome barriers.

The 1980s also marked the dawn of science-based concerns about the planet and how human activity impacts it—including pollution, deforestation, ozone depletion, and greenhouse emissions. In addition, there was a resurgence of interest in space that hadn't been seen since the late 1960s. NASA captured the nation's imagination with the successful launch of *Columbia* in 1982, ushering in the space shuttle era; it also experienced tragedy in 1986 when the space shuttle *Challenger* exploded just 73 seconds after takeoff, killing seven people.

That tragedy, however, didn't diminish the nation's optimism about scientific progress. In his speech on the *Challenger* disaster, President Reagan spoke directly to young people about the tragedy:

> I want to say something to the schoolchildren of America who were watching the live coverage of the shuttle's takeoff. I know it is hard to understand, but sometimes painful things like this happen. It's all part of the process of exploration and discovery. It's all part of taking a chance and expanding man's horizons. The future doesn't belong to the fainthearted; it belongs to the brave. The Challenger crew was pulling us into the future, and we'll continue to follow them.

It was an era before science became hyper-politicized—liberals and conservatives alike largely embraced it, seeing science and discovery as instrumental to our future as a nation and planet.

Tech Boom

This scientific renaissance was accompanied, not coincidentally, by a tech boom. Chapter 7 already explored the video game phenomenon—which began with arcades and Ataris, before evolving, around mid-decade into the near-ubiquitous Nintendo Entertainment System (NES) and eventually, the handheld Gameboy. But the 1980s also saw the birth of the personal computer, the mobile phone, the Walkman, the VCR, the VHS home video, and cable TV. These technologies completely transformed American life.

They changed the way we communicated, the way we watched movies and listened to music, and the ways people—especially young people—spent their time.

Not surprisingly, we see a number of these—and other—devices in *Stranger Things*. For example, Mike Wheeler can be seen sporting a calculator watch (which he later lends to Eleven to keep track of time). Long before smart watches, these classic multi-purpose watches caught fire with kids in the '80s. While they later became associated with nerds, in the mid-'80s, they were actually considered cool. Rock star Sting rocked the calculator watch on the cover of his single, "Wrapped Around Your Finger," as did Michael J. Fox in *Back to the Future.*

Perhaps the most prominent maker of the watches was Casio, though the version Mike wears, with five grey buttons across and four down (including a red "ON" button), seems to be a retro imitation watch rather than one from the actual period. According to prop master Lynda Reiss, the original plan was to have Mike wear a classic *E.T.* watch, but they couldn't afford the licensing rights.

Another popular device that makes an appearance in the show is the Sony Walkman. Before there were iPods, there were Walkmans—the first device to make music portable. The Walkman allowed people to listen to music on the go—while traveling, exercising, or taking a walk. It also allowed people to experience music privately. Once the headphones went on, no one—including parents—had to know what you were listening to. The Sony Walkman played a significant role in the music industry's renaissance in 1983, selling millions of copies as America shifted from vinyl to cassette tapes.

As much as it revolutionized music, however, the Walkman plays another role in *Stranger Things*. In Season 2, Chapter 3 ("The Pollywog"), Nancy brings home a RadioShack bag, which she tells her mom contains a replacement Walkman. That Walkman, as we see in the next episode ("Will the Wise"), turns out to be a Sony TCM-75V, a popular mid-'80s model. Rather than use it to play music, she stealthily uses it to tape record their interaction with Dr. Owens at Hawkins Laboratory to expose their culpability in the death of Barb.

The Walkman wasn't the only new way young people were listening to music in the '80s. The decade also saw the emergence of boomboxes—a portable stereo whose primary format was the cassette tape. Cassette tapes outsold records by 1983, becoming the most popular format for music for the remainder of the decade.

The first stereo we see in *Stranger Things* actually isn't a boombox, but a multi-format Fisher MC-4550 that features both a turntable and tape deck. That silver, wood-panelled stereo was originally released in 1981—one year prior to Jonathan's flashback, in which be blasts The Clash's "Should I Stay or Should I Go." The hybrid stereo makes sense for Jonathan as he likely had a sizable vinyl collection, but also clearly enjoys making mixtapes on cassette. In Will's room we also see a stereo, likely handed down from his older brother: a Panasonic RX-5090 boombox. That silver, single tape deck model with FM/AM radio was released in the late 70s. It appears in several scenes, most prominently when Will tries to communicate with his mother Joyce, from the Upside Down.

There are also a number of cameras in the show. Most prominent is Jonathan's high-end Pentax ME 35mm camera, which he uses to take pictures in the woods (and, of course, of Barb and Nancy at Steve's party). That camera would not have been cheap, which is, in part, what makes it so devastating when Steve destroys it. It might have taken over a year for Jonathan to save up to buy a new one. Fortunately, the much more affluent Nancy ends up gifting him a replacement camera (which appears to be the exact same model) at the end of Season 1, Chapter 8 ("The Upside Down").

In Season 2, we also see a number of cameras in Chapter 2 ("Trick or Treat, Freak") as the kids are getting ready for Halloween.

Among them is a vintage Polaroid "One Stop Flash" camera used by Karen Wheeler. Polaroid cameras exploded in the 1970s, selling up to 13 million cameras a year at their peak. The concept of an instantly produced picture was a novelty—in contrast to the typically arduous, lengthy process of waiting to get film developed, it happened before your eyes in seconds. You simply shook it and voila: a fully developed picture!

Polaroids remained widely used in the '80s. By the early 2000s, however, the landscape had changed and Polaroid filed for bankruptcy. More recently, though, there has been a resurgence of interest (similar to the resurgence of vinyl and other vintage media). In fact, Polaroid's head of global marketing, Martin Franklin, refers to the renewed interest as the *"Stranger Things* effect." "Thanks to *Stranger Things*," he explains, "people are enamoured by that 1970s and 1980s aesthetic…Our market research shows 18-to 24-year-olds are astonished the first time they see a Polaroid in action. It really hasn't lost its magic from 1972 when it debuted."

Beyond going to the arcade, we also know that the kids play Atari. The first Atari console—originally referred to as the Atari Video Computer System (VCS), and later renamed the Atari 2600— hit the market in 1977. However, given its high cost—$199 (which would be about $900 today, adjusted for inflation)—most families couldn't afford it. Still, around 250,000 units sold in its first year. Adjustments were made to the console to keep production costs down and reduce the price, and by 1979 it was selling over one million units, propelled by games like *Pong* and *Space Invaders*. For the next few years, the Atari became one of the most popular Christmas gifts. The wood-panelled console and joysticks became about as ubiquitous in American homes as boomboxes.

Although we never actually see the kids playing Atari in the show, we learn that both Dustin and Mike have consoles—although Mike's is taken away in Season 2, Chapter 1 ("MADMAX") as punishment for stealing his sister Nancy's money for the arcade. It's not clear if Lucas has one, but Will is hopeful that one is sitting under the Christmas tree in Season 1, Chapter 8 ("The Upside Down"). "It's definitely an Atari," he says giddily, "I felt Dustin's today and it's the same exact weight."

It's significant that Will—who comes from a much poorer home than Mike—is finally getting an Atari in 1983, when the price of the console had been cut dramatically. That year, in fact, marked the beginning of what is described as the "video game crash," in which the industry suddenly plummeted due to oversaturation and parental concerns. Will, however, can hardly be more excited to finally have his own Atari, and at around $99, it still represents a big sacrifice on the part of his single mother, Joyce.

And then there are the walkie talkies. Walkie talkies are about as central to *Stranger Things* as bikes. If bikes are symbols of childhood freedom, walkie talkies represent childhood communication. They represent an alternative wavelength, outside the purview of the adult world. They allow the kids to connect with each other—for ordinary contact, or for "code red" emergencies. They are even used to pick up signals from Will in the Upside Down.

The walkie talkies we see in the show seem to be realistic TRC-214 models released in the mid-1980s and sold at RadioShack. These models were not marketed towards kids, but rather for adults wanting stronger communication capability, perhaps for those working on a construction site or for outdoor excursions (camping or hiking). Featuring three channels and three watts, they would work pretty effectively up to a mile or so apart. They likely would have cost over a hundred dollars—pricey for middle-class kids in Hawkins.

But there's no doubt they come in handy. More than mere props, the walkie talkies play a crucial role in both seasons of the show. As tech journalist Jessica Conditt puts it: "These pieces of technology drive the story and shape the main characters on a fundamental level. They're not just nostalgia. They're necessary."

It is also part of what makes the show authentic. All of the science and technology props and references, from Carl Sagan to RadioShack to Apple computers to calculator watches, provide a sense of what it was actually like in the '80s. It doesn't hurt, of course, to have inspiring educational guides like Bob Newby and Mr. Clarke.

9

Food & Fashion

How connected are Eggo waffles with *Stranger Things*? Google "eggos" and the first suggested search association is *Stranger Things*. The brand, in fact, is now so associated with the show, it was featured at the beginning of a Super Bowl ad for *Stranger Things 2*. The 2017 commercial opens with a vintage Eggos commercial from the '80s, in which a brother and sister fight over a just-popped waffle in the toaster. "Leggo my eggo!" they say, reciting the brand's famous tagline. The nostalgia—about as thick as the syrup being slowly poured over the warm plate of waffles—is interrupted by Mike screaming, "Eleven!" and then a cut to the visuals for Season 2.

The commercial garnered a larger social media response than any other ad run during the Super Bowl that year. In fact, the Eggos social media account and *Stranger Things* account even playfully bantered with each other on Twitter. Yet this was not product placement in the traditional sense. According to Kellogg's (which owns the Eggo brand), it never paid for placement in the show—it was simply an organic plot (and character) device the Duffer Brothers came up with that worked. The frozen waffles were a staple of many households in the '80s—why not the Wheelers'? Kellogs certainly wasn't complaining.

The frozen waffles first make an appearance in the show in Season 1, Chapter 2 ("The Weirdo on Maple Street"), when Mike stuffs them in his jacket pocket, before sneaking them down to Eleven in the basement. "Got you breakfast," he says, handing her a waffle. Thereafter, the frozen waffles become an important symbol for El's character—and her relationship with Mike. It is the food she associates with friendship, belonging, home, love. It is, quite literally, comfort food.

There is an intentional irony about this as Eggo waffles are not exactly the gold-standard for an authentic home-cooked breakfast. They were invented in the 1950s as mass-produced frozen foods began to take hold in a marketplace increasingly driven by convenience. Making real waffles took time and effort; Eggos, by contrast, were quick and efficient—and left no mess behind. In the early 1970s, the brand was acquired by Kellogg's and debuted its famous slogan, "Leggo my Eggo." Its popularity exploded as it met demand from the rising number of single-parent and working-parent homes. By the 1980s, just about every family had a box of Eggos in their freezer.

It is no surprise, then, that the frozen waffles turn up in *Stranger Things*. What is surprising is how deftly the Duffer Brothers are able to weave the waffles into the story.

Eggos make their second significant appearance in Season 1, Chapter 6 ("The Monster"). Eleven finds herself alone and abandoned again—this time by her new friends after she was unable to help them find and save Will. After spending the night in the woods, she walks into a supermarket, dirty, disheveled, and hungry. Everyone stares. She feels their scrutinizing gaze, but marches forward resolutely, looking for something to eat. She finally sees something familiar in the frozen foods aisle: Eggo waffles. She quickly grabs several boxes (note the "Kids band together for safety" promo on the boxes).

The baffled store clerks call the police and try to stop her as she makes a b-line for the door. But Eleven is not having it, using her powers to block them with grocery carts and slamming the sliding glass doors shut behind her. The visual of her clutching several boxes of Eggos as the glass doors shatter behind her was indelible. It was the moment El's love of the frozen waffles was solidified, not only in the context of the show, but as a pop culture meme.

Eventually, Eleven makes her way back to the woods, where she gorges on the eggos by herself. It is in this episode we see that the frozen waffles mean more to her than just a random, vaguely cardboard-tasting food item. El remains a stranger in a strange land. As the title of the episode indicates, she feels like a monster, a freak. Without a home or family or friends, she seeks refuge in the comfort of Eggos because of what they represent—not only memories of Mike's kindness, but also of a brief moment where she had a place to call home.

In the final episode of Season 1 ("The Upside Down"), holed up at Hawkins Middle School, El and Mike are talking amongst themselves as Dustin and Lucas go looking for food, eventually discovering a fridge full of chocolate pudding. El has never heard of pudding, so Mike tries to explain what it is. He then tries to comfort her by telling her that she can live with him again once things settle down. She can have a place in his basement, he says, or even take his room.

"Don't worry," he reassures her, "when all this is over you won't have to keep eating junk food and leftovers like a dog anymore. My mom, she's a pretty awesome cook. She can make you anything you like."b"Eggos?" Eleven responds. "Well, yeah, Eggos," Mike says. "But real food too."

It is a great exchange—funny and moving—that once again highlights Eleven's difference and longing for normalcy. She doesn't understand the difference between "real food" and frozen, processed food because she's never had a normal life. To her, living in Mike's basement, eating Eggos sounds like heaven.

Toward the end of the episode, after the climactic encounter with the Demogorgon, in which Eleven seemingly sacrifices her life to save her friends, Eggos once again come into play—this time as Chief Hopper leaves some plastic-wrapped frozen waffles in a storage box in the woods. It is Christmas Eve—over a month since she disappeared—and snow now blankets the forest. But the Eggos are a cue to the audience that she may still be alive—or at least that Chief Hopper thinks she might be.

According to producer Shawn Levy, Eggos were not in the original script for this scene. "It was just going to be some food from the party," Levy revealed. "The Duffers and I were talking about the scene over dinner one night and together we hatched this idea of leaving the Eggos specifically just to hint who he might be leaving the food for, or the hope of who he would be leaving the food for. That was one of 50 decisions that you stumble into and they become defining moments."

While Eggos play the most prominent food role in the series, a number of other brands are featured in the show—including a product famously featured in *E.T.*: Reese's Pieces. When Dr. Owens asks Will what his favorite candy is during an examination at Hawkins Lab, Will cites the famous candy Elliot used to lure E.T. "Good call," responds Dr. Owens. "I'm more of a Mounds guy, but I've got to say, peanut butter and chocolate, it's hard to beat that."

The chocolate candy that actually plays a more *E.T.*-like role in *Stranger Things*, however, is 3 Musketeers. In Season 2, we see the candy bar in multiple episodes, in its appropriately vintage packaging—white with red and blue stripes, as opposed to the silver packaging we are more familiar with today.

Consisting of chocolate with a whipped nougat center, the 3 Musketeers bar first appeared in 1932. By the 1980s, however, it was much less popular than candy bars like Snickers, Twix, Baby Ruth, and Butterfingers. This point is driven home in the show as the boys are out trick-or-treating and Lucas complains about getting yet another 3 Musketeers from an old lady. "What's wrong with 3 Musketeers?" asks Dustin. "No one likes 3 Musketeers," says Mike. "Yeah, it's just nougat," agrees Will. "Just nougat?" Dustin retorts indignantly. "It is top three for me!"

Just as Eggos became inextricably attached to Eleven's character in Season 1, Three Musketeers subsequently play an important role for Dustin in Season 2. At the end of Chapter 2 ("Trick or Treat, Freak"), as he returns from trick-or-treating, he hears something rustling in the trash. It turns out to be the small, pollywog-like creature that Dustin adopts as a pet. Like Dustin, that pet loves 3 Musketeer candy bars. "You like nougat too, huh?" Dustin says, smiling as he watches the creature nibble on the pieces he drops inside the glass cage. He decides to name the slimy little creature D'Artagnan—Dart for short—after one of the three musketeers.

In addition to *E.T.*, Dustin's chocolate-based connection with Dart also elicited comparisons to *The Goonies*. In that movie, Chunk—a Dustin-like character—pacifies and befriends Sloth, the disfigured character held hostage by the Fratellis, with a Baby Ruth candy bar. Similarly, in the final chapter of Season 2 ("The Gate"), Dustin is able to pacify Dart, now no longer a cute creature, but a full-grown demodog, with a 3 Musketeers candy bar. The candy bar symbolizes their bond and allows he and his friends to escape unscathed. "Goodbye, buddy," he says, after feeding him the chocolate-coated nougat for the last time.

We see a number of other period-specific iterations of food brands. In Season 1, Chapter 3 ("Holly, Jolly"), Eleven is flipping through channels on TV in Mike's house when a Coca-Cola commercial comes on. That commercial actually premiered in 1983, the year Season 1 takes place. Seeing the ad, however, triggers an unpleasant memory for Eleven, in which she is being tested in Hawkins Lab. Dr. Brenner looks on approvingly, as she crushes a Coke can with her mind. But El looks scared and confused. When she awakes from the flashback, the commercial is still playing, concluding with soft drink's '80s tagline, "Coke is it!"

In the same episode, when the boys are preparing for "Operation Mirkwood" to save Will, Dustin brings a large assortment of snacks, including a number of '80s staples: Bazooka bubble gum, Smarties, Little Debbie Nutty Bars, Pringles, and Nilla Wafers. In Season 2, Chapter 1 ("MADMAX"), we see Keith, the awkward teenager who works at the arcade, chomping on an old-school bag of Cheetos. Meanwhile, in just about every breakfast scene (and there are many), we see the iconic figurine glass-bottle of Mrs. Buttersworth syrup. We also see Jiffy Pop popcorn—Joyce cooks the tin-wrapped package on the stove—in Season 2, Chapter 1 ("MADMAX"), as they get ready for movie night. The stove-top popcorn, which expanded the aluminum covering as it cooked, preceded microwave popcorn as the go-to option for families in the '80s.

In perhaps the funniest food scene, Steve and Nancy sit down to an awkward dinner with Barb's parents, the Hollands, in Season 2, Chapter 1 ("MADMAX"). Barb's mom, Mrs. Holland, apologizes for not having time to make a home-cooked meal, offering instead a spread from fast food chain Kentucky Fried Chicken. On the dinner table, we see the classic red and white-striped buckets of chicken, along with smaller plastic containers of mashed potatoes and coleslaw. While Mrs. Holland seems a bit embarrassed, Nancy and

Steve insist the meal is fine. "I love KFC," says Steve, graciously (some viewers point out that the company didn't officially change its name to KFC until 1991, although, in the show's defense, the initials *were* often used by customers before that).

The scene's incorporation of Kentucky Fried Chicken works not only because the company was so popular in the '80s, but also because of the way it highlights a national trend of families turning to fast food to compensate for their hectic work schedules. Over the course of the meal, Nancy and Steve learn that Barb's parents have put their house up for sale to pay for a private investigator to look into their daughter's disappearance. Disturbed by this development, Nancy excuses herself to go to the bathroom. Left alone with Barb's parents, Steve bites into a piece of fried chicken, and, not knowing what else to say, decides to repeat KFC's famous tagline: "This is finger-lickin' good." (Note: This is probably one of the Top 5 funniest moments in the series).

Fashion

Is there a good transition from food to fashion? Probably not. But they *are* both integral to the iconography of the show. Nothing in *Stranger Things*—not even Eggos—has inspired more memes than the singular fashion sensibility of Barb Holland.

Played by Shannon Purser in her debut screen role, Barb became an internet sensation, inspiring endless gifs, hashtags, and tributes. *Vulture* declared her the best character on the show. *The Daily Beast* referred to her as a "no-nonsense normcore queen." *Vanity Fair*, meanwhile, explained the phenomenon of Barb like this:

> There might be plenty of female misfits on TV nowadays, but most of them still *look* like Nancys: slender women with big eyes and porcelain skin. By contrast, the bespectacled,

freckle-flecked Barb looks more like someone you might actually meet in real life—or could have met, if you were around in the '80s. And for that, she's a singular presence on TV who has clearly struck a nerve.

After dying at the beginning of Chapter 3 ("Holly, Jolly")—*I warned there would be spoilers!*—viewers were (like Nancy) incensed that so little attention was given to her disappearance, particularly compared to Will. They demanded justice for Barb. The Barb obsession became so intense, Purser was forced to quit her job at a movie theater because too many fans wanted to meet her in person.

Purser was stunned by the response to her character. "The whole Barb phenomenon blew me away," she acknowledged. "Barb wasn't supposed to be a big deal and you lovely people made her important," she told her fans on Twitter. Even the Duffer Brothers admit they didn't see it coming, though they were thrilled it did. Like many others, they identified with Barb as someone on the outside looking in. "It was very easy for us to write the Barb character," said Ross Duffer, "and I think that, you know, Shannon Purser—who had never acted before—just did such a brilliant job realizing her. And, again, without very many lines—25 lines. And I think everyone feels like either they knew this girl or they were this girl."

Of course, Barb had some detractors. Some saw her character as sanctimonious and jealous or possessive of Nancy. Yet clearly, as *Vanity Fair* put it, she struck a nerve. And while there are, no doubt, many reasons for this, a big part of it had to do with her look.

Costume designer Kimberly Adams-Galligan's main goal for Barb—and the show's other characters—was authenticity. "The Duffer Brothers' biggest focus was that they wanted the characters to be real and not kitschy versions of what people remember of the '80s, which happens a lot," she said.

For Barb, the signature look included high-waisted, light-colored jeans (sometimes referred to as "mom jeans"); a high-necked plaid blouse (tucked in); and big, plastic-framed glasses (which some compared to those worn by Stef from *The Goonies*). "We tried lots of clothing," said Adams, "but when she put on that first ruffled plaid blouse, we both looked at each other and knew we had found her!"

Yet Barb's style was also about her short, red hair and freckles; her height and body type. As Purser herself wrote on Twitter. "Can I be super real? Didn't think a girl with my body type could get this far. I'm so thankful and excited." Matt Duffer believed this is part of why people connected with her. "I just think no one casts anyone like her. And that was something important to us and important to [casting director Carmen Cuba] was that we're casting kids and teens who feel very real… She looks like someone you might really go to school with."

Just as much care went into the costume design for other characters. Kimberly Adams—who oversaw costume design for Episodes 1-4—scoured '80s films and TV shows, as well as catalogs, magazines, and yearbooks from the period. Then she put together "mood boards" that established the look and feel of different characters or groups. For the Byers family, for example, she wanted to make sure the clothes didn't feel as new or in-style, consistent with their socio-economic circumstances. Will's clothes, accordingly, were intended to look like hand-me-downs, compared to Mike's newer outfits. Nancy Wheeler, meanwhile, wears a combination of preppy sweaters, turtlenecks, and cardigans—capturing her character's place somewhere in between cool girl and conscientious student. "Her family is upper middle class, she is smart and sweet and feminine and her closet needed to reflect that."

Along with Barb, perhaps the most iconic look from the show is Eleven—as dressed by the boys—in pink dress, navy blue windbreaker, and striped tube socks. The pink babydoll dress comes from Nancy's old wardrobe, while the jacket and socks seem to be from Mike's. That combination has already become one of the most popular Halloween costumes—with or without the blonde wig—and instantly recognizable as associated with *Stranger Things*.

For Season 2, Eleven's signature buzz cut is replaced with curly brunette locks, and her dress with more rustic baggy clothes, including overalls and heavy jackets. "In my head," explained new costume designer Kim Willcox, "Hopper had been giving her clothes he already had in boxes in his cabin, and then maybe making a run to the next county to go to a thrift store and buy stuff for a boy, as a disguise."

That look, of course, changes dramatically, in Chapter 7 ("The Lost Sister"). What was the inspiration for "punk Eleven"? "We wanted her to become part of the gang," explains Wilcox, "to absorb part of that look, to be this rougher person. So half of her costume is still made up of things she would've brought with her— her famous Converse, her socks, her jeans—but we felt that the top half would've been borrowed from the others, and that it'd be fun to combine a torn T-shirt with a tweedier element." The end result— with eye shadow, slicked-back hair, and dark blazer—is a look inspired by MTV stars like Madonna and the Bangles, as well as punk rockers like Siouxsie Sioux and Joan Jett.

Beyond Eleven and her new punk crew, Willcox wanted to make the clothes in Season 2 more vibrant—just as they gradually evolved over the course of the '80s. "I wanted to infuse more of the colors of the early '80s," she says, "so while we kept a lot of that earthy palette—the tans and browns and blues—we also added in some pastels and slightly poppier colors. The tones are a little happier-looking." We see these colors on the boys as well as the girls (colors weren't nearly as gendered in the '80s).

Season 2's newcomers also bring very distinct stylistic sensibilities. Max, the tomboy skater girl from California, wears a red-striped track jacket in one episode, and a bright yellow windsurfer sweatshirt in another. Her older brother Billy, meanwhile, is all denim: jean jacket, tight-fitting vintage Levi's, and boots. And, of course, the mullet. "I just love the moment when the Camaro first pulls out, his boot comes out of the car and hits the ground, and all the girls are staring," says Willox. "It's *so* '80s!" The inspiration for Billy's look came from a number of bad-boy figures from the '80s, but especially Rob Lowe's character (also named Billy) from *St. Elmo's Fire* (they even dawn the same earring).

Asked about her favorite costume design for Season 2, however, Willox picked a surprisingly subtle character—the normcore icon of the second season, Bob Newby. For his look, Willox "pulled up all these old photos of actual RadioShack employees [as inspiration]. They didn't really wear uniforms, usually just a suit or a sport coat and slacks. And a lot of polyester! So that boring brown-on-tan [look]—we were just like, "this is it." His jeans are so '70s, too. Bob definitely hasn't changed his style in a very long time."

As great as the newcomers' fashion statements are, no discussion of style in *Stranger Things* would be complete without mentioning Steve Harrington. Steve's look is vintage '80s prep: polo shirts, Levi's, khakis, pristine Nikes, Tom Cruise-like sunglasses. This makes sense as we not only know that Steve comes from a wealthy family (he has a heated pool!), he is also the prototypical "popular guy from high school."

But the real key to Steve's look is the hair. Steve seems to pull off that long, thick, voluminous hair effortlessly. Yet in a conversation with Dustin in Season 2, Chapter 6 ("The Spy"), while walking down the train tracks with Dustin, we learn the real secret: Fabergé Organics. "Use the shampoo and conditioner," he explains. "And when your hair is damp—it's not wet, okay? it's *damp*—do four puffs of the Farrah Fawcett spray." Dustin finds that revelation hilarious. "Farrah Fawcett spray?" "Yeah," Steve responds. "Farrah

Fawcett spray. You tell anyone I just told you that, and your ass is grass."

Perhaps the biggest style icon of the 70s, Farrah Fawcett signed a multi-million dollar endorsement deal with Fabergé Organics in 1977, shortly after starring in *Charlie's Angels*. Both the shampoo and hairspray were enormously popular in the late 70s and early '80s. Commercials for the product, featuring Fawcett, ran regularly on TV. The Duffers wanted to run one of those commercials in the show, but weren't able to get the licensing. "We wanted Eleven to see a Farrah Fawcett hair commercial early on when she was watching TV," said Matt Duffer, "but we just couldn't nail down the rights to it. Usually we can get it, but that one was one where we failed to lock it down." By the early '80s, Fawcett was no longer in the commercials anyway—in her place, was actress and model Heather Locklear.

Inspired by Steve's hair tips, Dustin is later seen using the Farrah Fawcett spray in preparation for the Hawkins Middle School Snow Ball Dance. Dustin's version of "Steve hair," of course, turns out a bit different: a combination of a mullet, pompadour and jheri curl (in real life, it took a lot of gel). But Dustin's wet-curly look is classic '80s and he rocks it with style and confidence.

Throughout the series, the fashion mantra was simple: authenticity. "For the Duffers," explains Kimberly Adams, "it was so important to make the characters real and not feel like caricatures of the 80's." Like so many other ingredients in the show, it works so well because of its attention to detail—to clothes, brands, hairstyles, makeup, accessories. "Every detail makes a difference to each character, even if it never gets seen on screen."

10

The Outsiders

In Season 2, Chapter 1 ("MADMAX"), Jonathan stops in Will's room, and finds his younger brother drawing a picture titled "Zombie Boy." It's a self-portrait. Jonathan asks if someone called him that at school, but Will is reluctant to talk. He says he is tired of people treating him like he is going to break, like he's a freak. "You're not a freak," Jonathan says. "Yeah, I am," Will responds emphatically. "*I am.*"

Jonathan, of course, knows what that feels like. "You know what?" he tells Will. "You're right. You are a freak." But it's okay, he says. It's okay to not be normal, to not be like everyone else. "I'm a freak too," he says. It can be lonely, he acknowledges, but it can also make life more interesting. "The thing is," he says, "nobody normal ever accomplished anything meaningful in this world."

Bob's entrance seconds later challenges the logic of that statement (sometimes, as Bob later proves, "normal" people can do extraordinary things), but Will seems to get Jonathan's point. Being different is okay.

The 1980s was a paradoxical decade when it came to difference—particularly for boys. On the one hand, it was a decade that seemed more comfortable even than today with men defying traditional gender expectations. Just look at the pop stars on MTV in that decade: not just Bowie (who Jonathan references), but also Prince, Michael Jackson, George Michael, and just about every British new wave band.

Moreover, many movies from the decade featured boys who were sensitive, vulnerable, and different—for example, *E.T.* (Elliot), *The Goonies* (Mikey), *Karate Kid* (Danny), *Stand By Me* (multiple characters), and *The Outsiders* (multiple characters). Of course, the '80s were also the decade of macho action figures like Rambo, The Terminator, and Dirty Harry. But in the '80s, at least in pop culture, it was okay for guys to look, act, and be different.

Yet it could also not be okay, especially in more provincial, conservative towns. Take, for example, the case of Ryan White. From Kokomo, Indiana—a town not unlike the fictional Hawkins—White learned he had contracted HIV from a blood transfusion (White was a hemophiliac) in 1984. He was thirteen years old.

When he returned to school, he was treated terribly by some of his fellow students, who called him a "queer" and a "faggot." White was harassed, mocked, and bullied; obscenity-laced notes were left in his locker and home mailbox. People at school and church treated him like a leper. "It was really bad," recalls his mother, Jeanne White Ginder. "People were really cruel, people said that he had to be gay, that he had to have done something bad or wrong, or he wouldn't have had it. It was God's punishment, we heard the God's punishment a lot. That somehow, some way he had done something he shouldn't have done or he wouldn't have gotten AIDS."

White was given just six months to live when he was diagnosed with HIV in 1984. Yet he managed to live six more years and become one of the most important voices in educating the American public about AIDS. He died in 1990.

In addition to informing people about AIDS, White's story also spoke to persisting bigotry surrounding boys perceived as queer—whether because of sexual orientation or simply because of other differences. We see this bigotry surface over and over in *Stranger Things*, particularly with the Byers brothers—and especially with Will, a Ryan White-like figure who wants nothing more than to simply live a normal life.

I Know, It's Weird

Will's older brother Jonathan is perhaps the most obvious outsider in *Stranger Things*—the archetypal wounded, misunderstood introvert. It is clear from early in the show that Jonathan feels alienated in Hawkins, Indiana. It's not just his musical tastes. It's not just the insular town or the the way he's treated at school. It's not just his parents' divorce or the role he is forced to play at home in place of his absent father—note in Season 1, Chapter 2 ("The Weirdo on Maple Street") how he is making breakfast for the family and how he takes an extra shift to help them make ends meet). It is a combination of all of these things—and a general sense of buried pain that almost swallows him when his only real friend, his brother Will, goes missing.

Jonathan is quiet, introspective, and gentle, not qualities generally valued in the often-cruel, stratified world of high school. When we first see him in that environment in Chapter 2 ("The Weirdo on Maple Street"), he is putting up "missing" posters for his lost brother. The popular kids look on with a combination of contempt and amusement. "Oh, God, that's depressing," says Steve, while his friend Tommy speculates that Jonathan may have killed his brother himself. Only Nancy has the decency to show compassion and approach Jonathan, assuring him that Will will be okay.

But no one else seems to care. He is alone, invisible at school. His alienation is exemplified by his interest in photography. His camera allows him to interact with the world, but still remain somewhat detached from it. As he later explains to Nancy, "I guess I'd rather observe people, than, you know…" "Talk to them?" says Nancy, completing his sentence. "I know, it's weird," Jonathan says. But he explains that photography, to him, feels more authentic than everyday, superficial interactions. Nancy seems to understand.

But most people don't. In Chapter 3 ("Holly, Jolly"), Steve and his group of friends confront Jonathan after school about the photos he took in the woods. They steal his backpack, and begin sifting through the pictures. One girl calls them "creepy." Jonathan defends himself, saying he was just looking for his brother. "No," says Steve, "This is called stalking." When Nancy sees the photo he took of her undressing by the window, Jonathan is humiliated. Sensing this, Steve continues to push and label him a deviant. "That's the thing about perverts," he says, "It's hardwired into them, you know, they just can't help themselves." He proceeds to rip up the photo and shatter Jonathan's camera.

Alone in the World

Jonathan is also what some might describe pejoratively as "soft." He isn't aggressive with girls. He doesn't play sports. He doesn't like violence. It is implied that his father Lonnie was abusive—physically and emotionally. We learn, for example, that Lonnie tried to make him "more of a man" in a variety of ways, including forcing him to shoot and kill a rabbit at the age of ten, which Jonathan refused to do.

Jonathan seems to have a visceral disgust for his father and what he represents. Which is not say he is a wimp. At several points, he stands up forcefully to his father. And in Season 1, Chapter 6 ("The Monster"), he beats the hell out of Steve. That only comes, however, after Steve relentlessly pushes him past his breaking point. His first instinct is to simply get Nancy out of the situation safely. But Steve keeps taunting. He implies that Nancy is a "slut," and says he always thought Jonathan was a "queer." Then he attacks Jonathan's family, saying that his mother is such a "screwup" it is no wonder Will went missing.

That's when Jonathan turns around and delivers a colossal punch to Steve's face. He doesn't let up either—something inside him seems to have snapped—and he continues to assault Steve on the ground, until he is removed by a police officer. Later, in the police station, Flo tells Nancy: "Only love makes you that crazy, sweetheart...and that damn stupid."

Yet Jonathan's default mode is non-violent and gentle. In Season 1, Chapter 5 ("The Flea and the Acrobat"), for example, when he and Nancy come across the wounded deer in the forest, Jonathan tries to take charge, to be a man, and put the deer out of its misery. But seeing it lying there, bloody and whimpering, he can't bring himself to pull the trigger. Similarly, in Season 2, Chapter 8 ("The Mind Flayer"), as the demodogs are approaching the Byers house, Chief Hopper asks if Jonathan can use a rifle. Jonathan hesitates; it is Nancy who steps forward. "I can," she volunteers.

Jonathan is old enough that he has found ways to accept and, in some ways, exalt his outsider identity. In Season 1, Chapter 2 ("The Weirdo on Maple Street"), in the flashback where he's introducing Will to The Clash, he tells his younger brother not to worry about not going to a baseball game with his father. "He's trying to force you to like normal things," he says. "And you shouldn't like things because people tell you you're supposed to."

Yet this disaffected, outsider identity is occasionally punctured by those few people he allows in. In Season 1, Chapter 5 ("The Flea and the Acrobat"), when he tries to tell Nancy that she looked "alone" in the photo he took of her—like she was "trying to be someone else," she calls "bullshit." She is not trying to be someone else, she says. He just doesn't like Steve. "Don't take it so personally," says Jonathan. "I don't like most people. He's in the vast majority."

But Nancy's not having it. She was actually starting to think he was okay, she says, and "not the pretentious creep everyone says he is." The remark clearly hits close to home, as Jonathan responds defensively, puncturing Nancy's own sense of self in turn. In this way, they are actually good for each other: Jonathan compels her to actually think about what she wants out of life, while Nancy allows Jonathan to be less inward and isolated.

In Season 2, Chapter 2 ("Trick or Treat, Freak"), for example, when Jonathan tries to get out of going to a Halloween party, because he is taking Will trick-or-treating, Nancy calls him out. "No, no way," she says, "You're going to be home by eight, listening to the Talking Heads and reading Vonnegut or something." Jonathan shrugs. "That sounds like a nice night." Nancy, however, prevails in getting him out of his shell, and Jonathan ends up going to the party.

Jonathan's mother, Joyce, likewise, tries to get Jonathan not to isolate himself so much—to let people in. She recognizes he's had a difficult life in certain ways, and has always been good at taking care of himself. But she implores him not to cut her out, particularly in their joint effort to find Will. "This is not yours to fix alone," she tells him at the police station in Season 1, Chapter 7 ("The Bathtub"). "You act like you're all alone out there in the world. But you're not. You're not alone."

It is a powerful moment of solidarity between a broken mother and son. Joyce knows she often overlooks Jonathan for Will. But to rescue Will, they will need each other. Gradually, as the series progresses, Jonathan gets better at letting people in—not only his mother and Will, but also Nancy, Bob, and others.

Fairies in Fairyland

Will faces similar struggles because of his differences. Like Jonathan, he is soft and sensitive, which makes him an easy target for bullies. When he goes missing in Season 1, Chapter 1 ("The Vanishing of Will Byers"), his mother Joyce tries to explain this to Chief Hopper. He's not like other kids, she says. He has a few friends, but he is constantly bullied. "They're mean, they make fun of him, they call him names, they laugh at his clothes…" "What's wrong with his clothes?" Hopper asks. That's not the point, Joyce responds (though it does suggest their family's relatively low socioeconomic status is part of the equation). The broader point is that he never fit in. She confides that Will's now-estranged father, Lonnie, "used to say he was queer, called him a fag." "Is he?" asks Hopper. "He's missing is what he is," Joyce retorts.

Will may or may not actually be gay, but there is no question that is the perception in Hawkins. Like Ryan White, he is a magnet for homophobic epithets. When an assembly is held at Hawkins Middle School to honor him after his assumed death, he is praised as "an exceptional student, and wonderful friend." Yet his actual friends see the whole thing as phony. Most of the school never knew him, or cared about him. To the extent that they were aware of him, it was often to tease him. They even see a couple of kids laughing and snickering during the assembly. Fortunately, Will has a great group of loyal friends.

After the assembly, Mike confronts the boys he saw mocking Will. "You think this is funny? I saw you guys laughing over there. And I think that's a real messed up thing to do." "What's there to be sad about?" responds Troy, one of the bullies. "Will's in fairyland now, right? Flying around with all the the other fairies. All happy and *gay*."

Usually not one for physical confrontation, Mike stands up for Will, pushing Troy to the ground. Then, just as Troy is about to attack Mike, Eleven uses her powers to make Troy pee his pants. It is a great moment of vindication, not only for Will, but the entire group.

We Stick Together

The ragtag group of misfits and outsiders, as explored in previous chapters, was a classic '80s trope, from *It*, to *The Goonies*, to *Stand By Me*. In the case of *Stranger Things*, in addition to Will (and later Eleven), we have Mike, who is awkward and nerdy, Lucas, who seems to be one of the only black kids in Hawkins, and Dustin, who has cleidocranial dysplasia, a rare condition that affects the development of bones and teeth (Gaten Matarazzo, who plays Dustin, revealed that he also has the condition in real life and has tried to use his platform to education the public about it). These boys don't play sports or run for student council; they play Dungeons and Dragons and belong to the AV Club. They are, as Lucas's sister Erica succinctly puts it, a "bunch o' nerds."

And along with Will, they are all susceptible to bullying. In Season 1, Chapter 1 ("The Vanishing of Will Byers"), when the boys pull up to school on their bikes, they are immediately confronted by James and Troy, their archenemies. "Step right up, ladies and gentlemen," says Troy. "Step right up and get your tickets to the freak show." He proceeds to assign each of them a disparaging nickname: Midnight (Lucas), Frogface (Mike), and Toothless (Dustin). James, the other bully, mimics Dustin's lisp, before forcing him to perform for their amusement. "Assholes," says Lucas, after they've left.

Such confrontations persist throughout Season 1. In Chapter 3 ("Holly, Jolly"), Troy and James sneak up on the gang in the school yard and mock them about their missing friend. "You know what my dad said," taunts Troy, "he said he was probably killed by some other queer." Mike tells Lucas and Dustin to just ignore them, and begins walking away. James, however, trips him, and he falls to the ground, cutting his chin.

His friends, however, have his back, just as he has theirs. When Dustin is mocked for his cleidocranial dysplasia, Mike builds him back up—"it's like a superpower. Like Mr. Fantastic or something." As mentioned earlier, Mike also stands up for Will at the assembly.

Dustin, meanwhile, often plays the role of mediator or peacemaker in the group. After the altercation between Mike and Lucas at the junkyard, in which Eleven accidentally knocked Lucas unconscious it is Dustin that convinces Mike to apologize for drawing first blood. "All three of you were being a bunch of little assholes!" he says. "I was the only reasonable one." Dustin is not afraid to be blunt, but his core quality as a friend and person is loyalty. As he puts: "We stick together, no matter what."

While there are occasional rifts, the group does just that when it counts. One of the most impressive displays of solidarity comes in Season 1, Chapter 6 ("The Monster"). Seeking payback for the assembly incident, Troy and James ambush Dustin and Lucas in the woods. The boys drop their bikes and flee, but are eventually cornered against a cliff. Troy pulls a knife on Dustin, and demands to know how they made him pee his pants. "I know you did something to me, some nerdy science shit to make me do that."

"Our friend has superpowers," declares Dustin, "and she squeezed your tiny bladder with your mind." Troy doesn't find that explanation funny, and threatens to cut out the rest of his "baby teeth" unless Mike jumps off the cliff, into the lake, hundreds of feet below. Dustin pleads with Mike not to do it, as he could very possibly die. But Mike bravely steps to the edge of the cliff, looks down, takes a deep breath, and jumps.

Mike, of course, is ultimately saved by Eleven in one of the season's most epic scenes. Yet this moment also shows how loyal these boys are to each other, especially when it's needed most.

Stay Away From Him

The storyline of Season 1, in fact, is driven, in many ways, by the boys' relentless dedication to finding their lost friend. Often overlooked in his remarkable commitment to that mission is Lucas. Lucas is a realist, a pragmatist. He is understandably skeptical about Eleven, who he calls "the Weirdo," because he believes she is a distraction from their real goal, which is to find Will. Eventually, frustrated by Mike's refusal to renounce Eleven, he resolves to find the gate himself.

In Season 1, Chapter 6 ("The Monster"), we see him gathering together a backpack full of supplies, including a compass, walkie talkie, and binoculars, and tying on a camouflage headband, Rambo-style, before heading out on his bike. He is led to the fence surrounding Hawkins Lab, where he climbs a tree and spies on activities around the building with his binoculars.

It is this resourcefulness that alerts him to the culpability of Hawkins Lab in Will's disappearance—and the threat they now pose to the rest of the group, especially Eleven. At the beginning of Chapter 7 ("The Bathtub"), Lucas frantically warns Dustin and Mike that "the bad men are coming," allowing them to escape out the side door of the Wheelers' house before the agents arrive. An epic bike chase scene ensues, punctuated by Eleven's heroic van-flip. This moment finally allows Lucas to see she is on their side. Back at the junkyard, he kneels down next to her, looks her in the eyes and apologizes. "Everything I said about you being a traitor and stuff...I was wrong," he says, putting his hand on her shoulder. "I'm sorry."

Throughout Season 1, we see different sides of Lucas's personality: he can be both stubborn and intrepid, courageous and humble. In Season 2, however, we get a better sense of his character as some of the racial realities in suburban Indiana emerge.

The first explicit acknowledgement of race in the series comes in a more lighthearted moment as the group banters about who was supposed to dress up as Venkman from *Ghostbusters* for Halloween. Mike says that Lucas was supposed to be Winston—an African American character who plays more of a supporting role in the movie. But Lucas insists he didn't agree to that. "He joined the team super late, he's not funny, and he's not even a scientist." Mike responds that Winston is still cool. Why doesn't he dress up as him then, asks Lucas. Mike begins to stammer some excuse. "B-b-b-because you're not black," says Lucas. "I didn't say that," responds Mike. "You thought it," counters Lucas.

It's a funny exchange that also manages to make an important point: that Lucas, unlike Winston from *Ghostbusters*, is not content to be the token "minority" in the group, or play a minor role. Mike assumes that he gets to be the most popular and important member of the *Ghostbusters* team, but Lucas doesn't accept the terms of his logic. He refuses to be marginalized to a minor player just because of his race.

The scene also foreshadows the active role Lucas plays in the group as the rest of the season unfolds. Far from being a token, he actively takes things into his own hands. The best example of this is his evolving relationship with newcomer Maxine. When the group first learns of her, they are all, in typical adolescent fashion, paralyzed by inaction, confined to simply watch her from a distance (Max calls it "stalking").

Lucas and Dustin finally summon the courage to introduce themselves and invite her to go trick-or-treating. But of all the boys in the party, Lucas is the one who is able to earn her trust (by being honest) and make her feel included. Dustin, of course, is also enamored with the red-headed skater from California. But Lucas ultimately wins her heart by following his father's advice, and putting himself out there (Dustin follows Steve's advice to pretend like he doesn't care, which ultimately doesn't work as well).

Smartly, however, *Stranger Things* demonstrates that a relationship between a white girl and a black boy in a small town in the '80s was no straightforward matter. Before Max and Lucas even become close, Lucas comes under the crosshairs of Max's older step-brother, Billy. The Duffers acknowledged that Billy was intended to not only to be an abstract "human antagonist," but an actual racist whose "overall rage at the world" manifests via bigotry and violence. Lucas's relationship with Max allowed them "to be honest about what an [interracial] relationship like that would do, and how certain characters would react, and how a character like Billy would really react to that."

We see numerous examples of that throughout Season 2. In Chapter 4 ("Will the Wise"), for example, Billy sees Max talking to Lucas after school and stares him down menacingly. When Max gets in the car, he demands to know who the boy is. She tries to play it down, saying he is just some kid from class, but Billy doesn't believe her. He grabs her by the arm. "Something you learn is that there are certain types of people in this world that you stay away from," he tells her. "And that kid, Max, that kid, is one of them. You stay away from him, you hear me." A terrified Max is left in tears.

Billy's violent rage about his step-sister seeing a black boy persists throughout Season 2. In Chapter 5 ("Dig Dug"), he again threatens her after catching her talking to Lucas at the arcade. Still, in spite of the dangers, Lucas doesn't give up on Max. In Chapter 6

("The Spy"), he rides his bike to her house and rings the doorbell—a risky move to say the least. Fortunately, Max opens the door. But the tension is palpable. For Lucas, Billy is as dangerous as any Demogorgon. His friendship with Max is fraught with peril. When Billy walks over to answer the door, you can feel that. Thankfully, Max ends the conversation just in time, telling Billy that it was just Mormons at the door, before returning to her room. Once the coast is clear, she climbs out the window, and sneaks off with Lucas on his bike.

Billy finally catches the couple together at the Byers house in Chapter 9 ("The Gate"). It is a chilling moment. He first confronts Max. "I thought I told you to stay away from him," he tells her. He then turns to Lucas, picks the much smaller boy up by his shirt, and slams him into the wall. Max and the rest of the party look on, horrified, but seemingly helpless against Billy's rage. Lucas looks terrified too, but somehow manages sneak a kick to Billy's groin, destabilizing him enough for Steve to jump into the fray again.

Steve gets in a few good punches, but is subsequently beaten to nearly an inch of his life. An alert and courageous Max, however, finds one of Will's syringes with a needle and stabs it into Billy's neck. Stunned, Billy turns to attack her, but before he can, the drug begins to take effect, and he collapses. Max grabs the nail-riddled bat and stands over him. "From here on out, you leave me and my friends alone," she says. "Do you understand?"

In this way, Lucas and Max's relationship is a triumph over racism and bigotry. Seeing them together at the Hawkins Middle School Snowball Dance at the end of Season 2 is a moving scene, not just because they like each other and have a moment, but because of what that moment represents. It took a great deal of persistence, vulnerability and courage on both character's parts. And for the show, it represents a much more complete and aware picture of '80s

America than any John Hughes film (in which race is completely ignored).

Will the Wise, Mike the Empath

Another overlooked, but significant relationship in Season 2 is between Will and Mike. Will was already perceived as different at the beginning of Season 1, largely, we learn, because of the perception that he was "queer." But in Season 2, his difference is further amplified because—for most of his classmates—he was assumed dead, and now has returned from the dead. When he comes back to school, he feels even odder than he did before. People stare at him as he walks down the hallway. Cruel notes are left in his locker. He is called "zombie boy" and "freak." Much like Ryan White, he is viewed as a pariah, a leper.

Moreover, we learn early in Season 2 that Will is having frequent psychosomatic "episodes" in which he sees and feels things that others do not. He is being treated for these episodes at Hawkins Lab, but for much of the season, the doctors aren't sure how to diagnose or treat what he is experiencing. As the season unfolds, his episodes become more frequent and vivid. Not only does he suddenly find himself alone and frantic, in the Upside Down; he also has visions of an encroaching "shadow monster."

He tells Dr. Owens that this shadow monster makes him feel "frozen" with fear—that its presence is overwhelming. To deal with his anxiety, Will turns to art, drawing pictures of its tentacle-like form looming in a cloud-filled sky. His drawings make it more tangible and concrete. They are, in fact, the "evidence" that allows his mother to see that what he is experiencing is not just in his head. Eventually, they also save lives, serving as a visual representation of his spreading "now memories" and a map of the artery-like underground tunnels in Hawkins.

Many people try to help Will—his mother Joyce, Dr. Owens, Jonathan, Bob, his friends—but they aren't sure how. No one really understands what he's going through. They assume it has to do with post-traumatic stress, or perhaps even his family's history of mental illness. In Season 2, Chapter 3 ("The Pollywog"), Bob tries to help Will by confiding about his own childhood fears. He finally overcame them, he says, by standing up to them.

While offered with the right intentions, however, Bob's advice ultimately hurts Will even more. In the midst of a bad episode, Will runs outside the school into the field. But then he remembers what Bob told him and stops. He tries to be brave and "stand his ground." He shouts at the shadow monster to "go away." But instead of relenting, the creature reaches down his throat, consuming him entirely. When his mom and friends find him, he seems to be having a seizure, shaking uncontrollably in a trance-like state. Thereafter, he is completely infected. The monster—like a virus—is inside him. He tells his Mom that he tried to resist, but now "felt it everywhere. *Everywhere*."

It doesn't go away. In subsequent episodes, Will becomes the "host" for the shadow monster, connected by a hive mind. When the Upside Down is torched, it feels like he is being burned inside. When the shadow monster wants something—or wants him to do something—it seems impossible to resist.

Understandably, through most of Season 2, Will is not just "very sensitive," as Lucas describes him; he is on the verge of a breakdown. The friend who seems to best understand this is Mike. Where other people see Will as a freak, Mike sees him as special— not unlike Eleven. Mike believes Will has "true sight"—meaning he can see other dimensions regular people cannot. When Mike goes to check on his friend in Chapter 5 ("Dig Dug"), Will confirms as much. But he tells Mike that it no longer simply feels like he's in the Upside

Down; "It's like I feel what the Shadow Monster is feeling, see what he is seeing."

Sensing Will's dread, Mike suggests that maybe this could be a good thing. It means Will can spy on the creature and know what it is going to do. "If you know what he's seeing and feeling, maybe that's how we cans stop him," says Mike. Will remains uncertain, but Mike steadies his trembling hand, and assures him it will be okay. Throughout Season 2, Mike remains steadfast and loyal to his ailing friend.

Significantly, even as Will's memory begins to deteriorate, forgetting who Chief Hopper and Dr. Owens are, he still remembers Mike. In Chapter 8 ("The Mind Flayer"), Mike reminds Will of of when they first became friends. It was the first day of kindergarten. Neither of them had any friends. But then they found each other by the swing set. If Will's gift is "true vision," Mike's gift is that he can feel what others feel. He is an empath, a comforter. Just as he offered Eleven an emotional "home" in Season 1, in Season 2, he serves as an anchor for Will. He listens to Will, and makes him feel understood and accepted. To the rest of the school, Will may be queer, freak or "zombie boy," but to Mike he is "Will the Wise."

Redemption of the Douche

And then there's Steve Harrington. It seems strange to mention Steve in a chapter about outsiders. In many ways, he is the quintessential insider: popular, handsome, wealthy, athletic. Steve may never be an outsider in the same way as the other boys. But he does undergo a significant transformation, one in which he renounces his place with the cool kids and begins to identify with—and help—the marginalized.

Steve's metamorphosis begins near the end of Season 1. In Chapter 7 ("The Bathtub"), we see him hanging out with his friends,

Tommy and Carol, outside a gas station, still recovering from the beating he took from Jonathan (and Nancy's rejection). The incident, however, seems to have triggered some self-reflection. He calls Tommy and Carol out for slut-shaming Nancy just because she's not "miserable" and cruel like them. The conversation nearly devolves into a fistfight, but Steve seems to realize it's not worth it—and more importantly, they're not worth it as friends.

The next time we see him he is at the movie theater, volunteering to clean up the epithets spray-painted by his former friends on the marquee. In Chapter 8 ("The Upside Down"), he finds Nancy with Jonathan at the Byers' house and tries to apologize. Nancy, however, has bigger concerns —concerns that Steve suddenly becomes aware of when a Demogorgon breaks through one of the walls.

The decision Steve makes not to leave (after Nancy gives him an out), but stay and fight—nail-bat and all—alongside Nancy and Jonathan marks his decisive turn as a character. With Jonathan immobilized on the ground and Nancy out of bullets, Steve re-enters the house and attacks the the Demogorgon with a vengeance, picking up the nail-bat and swinging in an adrenalin-fueled barrage. Eventually, the Demogorgon is subdued, led into a trap, and lit on fire. Steve Harrington, one-time self-centered douche, has become a hero.

According to the Duffer Brothers, this wasn't the original plan. Steve was supposed to be the stereotypical cruel jock, but Joe Keery ended up injecting the character with such likeability and nuance that the script was changed. Ultimately, instead of having his character killed off—the original plan—he was given a redemptive arc, surprising cast members and viewers alike.

In Season 2, the transformation continues, as Steve takes on the role of full-time babysitter. Over the first few episodes, it becomes apparent that Steve is no longer the bigshot he once was. We see his insecurity about his academic abilities and post-high school plans. We see his alienation from his old friends. Moreover, it becomes increasingly clear that Nancy has moved on, growing closer to Jonathan as they embark on a journey to get to the bottom of Barb's death. Rather than grow jealous and angry, however, Steve accepts it, taking on a new role—and identity—as big brother to the kids, especially Dustin.

Dustin and Steve first meet up in Chapter 5 ("Dig Dug"). Dustin is at the Wheelers, looking for Mike, when Steve pulls up with a bouquet of roses for Nancy. Dustin, however, informs Steve that Nancy's not there—and in any case, they've got bigger problems than his "love life."

With that, they hop in Steve's maroon BMW, and the Steve-Dustin buddy tandem begins. Still a bit skeptical about Steve after Season 1, viewers of the show gradually began succumbing to Steve's charm over the course of Season 2. *Vice* declared his character's evolution "the *Stranger Things* transformation no one saw coming," while *Vanity Fair* wrote that he had become a new fan favorite." Meanwhile, Babysitter Steve and Dad Steve went viral as memes on social media.

Perhaps the moment that best exemplified his new role comes in Chapter 6 ("The Spy") as Steve and Dustin walk down the train tracks. "That's probably one of my favorite scenes," acknowledges Joe Keery, "because, for the first time in doing that, Steve lets his guard down. You can tell that these two characters, although they've been shoved together because they've been ditched by their friends, end up caring about each other and looking out for each other. It turns into this big-brother relationship, even though they're both a little stubborn and think they're the boss and they've got it all figured out. Underneath, there's this genuine care for each other. And that's what makes this relationship cool, that these two characters you wouldn't necessarily think would ever even interact, the fact that they bond over not having anyone else is what makes it special."

The train-track scene is the full manifestation of the new Steve: grounded, decent, and funny. He gives Dustin relationship advice, shares his hair secrets, and, instead of expressing bitterness about Nancy or calling her a "bitch," acknowledges that she is special.

In the ensuing episodes, Babysitter Steve becomes champion of the outsiders, fending off demodogs and bullies alike. In Chapter 6 ("The Spy") when he leaves the bus in the junkyard to protect the kids from the surrounding demodogs and use himself as bait, Max says, "He's insane." Dustin responds: "He's awesome."

In the final chapter ("The Gate"), Steve again stands up for the kids, this time to Billy Hargrove. When Billy rolls up in his Camaro, Steve meets him outside and does his best to diffuse the situation. It doesn't take long, however, before Billy has him on the ground, rolling over in pain. Yet just as in Season 1, Steve refuses to back down. As Billy slams the much younger and smaller Lucas to the wall, Steve returns and lands several good punches, before being knocked unconscious. While he can't save them in this instance (Max ultimately does the honor by shoving a needle in her brother's neck), the kids appreciate the attempt. As Dustin puts it to a groggy and mangled Steve in the back of the car: "He kicked your ass, but you put up a good fight."

Steve takes a beating for his transformation—literally and figuratively. But in the process, he becomes a better person— someone the kids look up to and trust. As Steve tells Nancy, "I may be a pretty shitty boyfriend. But it turns out I'm actually a pretty damn good babysitter."

11

———————

A Hero's Journey

Eleven is called many things over the first two seasons of *Stranger Things*: El, Jane, kid, weirdo, freak, mage, wizard, weapon, Russian spy, monster.

One thing is certain: she is one of the most memorable characters—from television or film—in recent history. With her signature buzz cut, pink dress, tube socks, and bloody nose, Eleven quickly became an icon. With her remarkable telekinetic powers and legendary acts, she also became a cult hero—a new generation's Luke Skywalker or Harry Potter.

Played by Millie Bobby Brown, Eleven speaks a grand total of 246 words in Season 1. Yet she managed to inject the scenes she appeared in with such presence, subtlety, and force, that the unusual lab refugee she played somehow felt fully inhabited, *real*. Overnight, then-12-year-old Millie went from obscure, struggling young actress to global phenomenon.

Eleven, of course, is not the only remarkable female character from the show. Joyce Byers, played by veteran A-lister Winona Ryder, delivers a pitch-perfect performance as a strong, tenacious mother determined to find—and in Season 2, protect—her son. One of the first actors cast in the show, Winona Ryder was best known prior to *Stranger Things* for her work in the late '80s and 90s, including acclaimed roles in *Beetlejuice* (1988), *Edward Scissorhands* (1990), *Little Women* (1994), and *The Crucible* (1996). With her short hair and expressive brown eyes, she often played roles that balanced innocent ingenue with eccentric rebel. In Joyce, we see Ryder's characteristic passion and kinetic energy but in a new kind of role: a single mother struggling to make ends meet, take care of two sons, and maintain her grip on reality.

Nancy Wheeler (played by Natalia Dyer), similarly, is a strong, dynamic character whose relentless pursuit of the truth eventually delivers justice for Barb. Rather than simply fall into the predictable stereotype of the pretty, popular girl, Nancy is, as Steve puts it after losing her, "different." She is smart—not just book smart—she is an independent thinker; she has a mind of her own. She is also brave, frequently standing up to people or taking control of situations when others are too tepid. And she is compassionate. She reaches out to Jonathan after his brother disappears; she dances with Dustin when no one else will; and she refuses to allow her best friend to die in vain.

There are a number of other great female characters, including Max Mayfield (played by Sadie Sink), the red-headed California tomboy who arrives—and enthralls the boys with her video game prowess and acerbic wit—in Season 2; Barb (played by Shannon Purser), the loyal friend and confidante whose journey ends much too soon (Barb's character is discussed in more depth in Chapter 9); and Karen Wheeler (played by Cara Buono), who, in addition to perfectly capturing the '80s suburban mom, has one of the best scenes in the show (with Billy in Season 2, Chapter 9—you know the one).

These female characters are a big part of what make the show so compelling—and so different than the typical male-dominant ensembles we usually see in science fiction and coming-of-age adventures. Women aren't just featured as supporting characters; they play instrumental roles. Leading this incredible female cast is Eleven—the breakout star of the show.

Rule the World

As noted in Chapter 3, Eleven bears some strong resemblances to supernatural female characters from the 1970s and '80s, particularly Stephen King's Carrie White (from *Carrie*) and Charlie McGee (from *Firestarter*).

Yet more broadly, she also feels right at home amongst the fierce, eccentric, gender-bending female icons of the '80s. The '80s are often described as an era in which women began to face a backlash for the inroads they had made since the 1960s. Traditionalists worried that women had become *too* liberated. In the media, debates raged about sex and the body, family roles, and careers.

In her bestselling 1984 novel, *The Handmaid's Tale* (which was recently adapted into a popular Hulu series starring Elisabeth Moss), Margaret Atwood imagined a future dystopian society in which women have suddenly lost basic rights and are treated as property of a male-dominated theocratic state. Many read it as a critique of the rising Religious Right and its call for a return to traditional values, particularly for women.

Yet while there was undoubtedly a powerful conservative current in regards to women's roles, the '80s also saw the rise of a new generation of women who refused to accept any kind of box or ceiling. In an interview with Dick Clark on American Bandstand in 1983, pop star Madonna famously declared her intention to "rule the world." That kind of ambition for women was long considered taboo.

But artists like Madonna expressed a new kind of comfort and confidence with being who they wanted to be and going after what they wanted in life. In 1990, cultural critic Camille Paglia declared her the "future of feminism."

The '80s was also the era of Jane Fonda's fitness revolution and Sandra Day O'Connor's ascent to the Supreme Court. It was an era in which Princess Leia (played by the incredible Carrie Fisher) was not content to be a damsel in distress, nor was Sigourney Weaver's action hero Ripley in *Alien*. It was an era in which unique, quirky women like Cyndi Lauper and Molly Ringwald became cultural icons, artists like Annie Lennox and Sinead O'Connor rocked buzz cuts and challenged conventions, and African American artists like Janet Jackson and Whitney Houston broke records and shattered barriers.

The '80s, that is, set the stage for what Millie Bobby Brown described at the 2017 MTV Movie and TV Awards as the "badass, female, iconic character" she plays in *Stranger Things*.

Discovering Eleven

When Millie Bobby Brown auditioned for *Stranger Things*, she was, ironically, eleven years old. Born in Spain to British parents, Millie grew up in England, before moving to Orlando at the age of seven to chase her dream of being an actress. While she had no prior training or acting experience, she managed to land an agent and several small roles in shows like *Once Upon a Time in Wonderland*, *Modern Family*, and *Grey's Anatomy*. Her first major role came in the BBC show, *Intruders*, a 2014 sci-fi drama; however, that show failed to gain traction among critics or viewers and was canceled after one season.

Then came the *Stranger Things* audition in 2015. At the time, Millie confesses, she'd just about lost hope in getting her big break.

But then, out of the blue came, the opportunity of a lifetime. Millie nailed her *Stranger Things* audition and got a callback

The Duffer Brothers were intimately involved in the casting process. "We had five kids [we needed for the series]," says Matt Duffer, "and we knew that even one [bad child performance] would really hurt the show. Shawn knew that, we knew that, Netflix knew that. So the minute they greenlit the show, and at this point we only had one script written at the time, we started a very intensive worldwide search for these kids. When you boil it down, we saw about a thousand kids in total. And when you boil it down, there's so few that can operate at this level that it was instantly clear to everyone which were our kids, and which kids could actually do this show." Especially crucial was the role of Eleven, which they knew had the unique challenge of carrying a lead performance with almost no dialogue.

Producer and director Shawn Levy praised the Duffers' insistence on getting the casting right. "Even when we saw dozens of talented kids the Duffers insisted on continuing the search until they found the authenticity that they were looking for," he recalls. "And that dogged persistence was incredible and requires tremendous confidence for new filmmakers."

The persistence paid off. After a few separate auditions, which included acting out parts from classic '80s movies like *Stand By Me*, Millie got the part. The Duffers could tell she was a special talent. She had a certain authenticity and intensity that was rare for a child actor. She didn't feel Disney-fied; she felt natural, real. Shawn Levy remembers her unveiling her signature stare in one of the auditions. "I've never forgotten it, because it was so intuitive," recalls Shawn Levy. "That this little person had such fierce power—that's what took me aback."

After securing the role, however, Millie was informed of one provision: she would have to shave her head. Millie's parents were initially concerned; however, the Duffers convinced them—and Millie—that it was not only necessary for the part, but could actually be empowering. They showed her photos of Charlize Theron from *Mad Max: Fury Road* (2015), who similarly buzzed her hair for the role, for which she won a Critics Choice Movie Award for Best Actress. She could play a similarly "badass" role, the Duffers said. Millie—and her parents—decided to sign off. "It was the best decision I've ever, ever made," recalls Millie.

To prepare for the role, Millie was instructed to watch a number of '80s classics, including *Poltergeist*, *Stand By Me*, and *The Goonies*. But most importantly, they wanted her to study the tone and dynamics of Spielberg's 1982 masterpiece, *E.T.* Her character, like E.T., would be like a lost alien in a foreign world.

Production for *Stranger Things* took about six months. While they knew Millie was special before filming commenced, it wasn't until they were in the trenches that they realized how special. "Child actors, even the great ones, almost always have difficulty *listening*," remarked the Duffers. "They're able to deliver their lines well, but to stay fully in character in a scene when they're not talking… that's another skill set entirely." Millie not only had that skill set, she had what the Duffers described as "a downright spooky preternatural talent. She inhabits every moment so intensely, with some alchemy of intelligence, preparation, and instinct. By the end of production, we found ourselves listening to Millie as if she were one of our most seasoned adult actors."

Her fellow actors were similarly impressed, from her fellow kid crew to seasoned veterans like Winona Ryder and David Harbour, the latter of whom stated that he believed she had the potential of a Meryl Streep. "We have yet to give her something that she's unable to do," said show co-creator Matt Duffer. "I can throw this girl an incredible fastball, she's going to hit it. It's like a singer who can hit any note. Her range is just absolutely incredible. I have yet to see any limits to it."

When the series hit Netflix in the summer of 2016, the rest of the world got to see what they were seeing on set. *Vanity Fair* called her screen presence "commanding," particularly highlighting her on-screen chemistry with Finn Wolfhard (Mike). *The New Yorker* described her role in the show as a "career-launching performance...Her head shaved, her face grave, she's silent for much of the series, but she bends the story toward her, through fearless emotional transparency." Meanwhile, when bestselling novelist Stephen King tweeted his admiration for the show, he single out Millie's performance as "terrific." "Is it my imagination," he wrote, "or are child actors a lot better than they used to be?"

It didn't take long after the show premiered for Millie Bobby Brown to become a household name. Within a matter of months, her character become one of the most popular Halloween costumes that fall, with thousands of fans posting photos on social media. According to clothing retailer Lyst, search data found huge spikes in interest for "pink collar dresses," "tube socks," and "blue jackets." According to IMBD, the online movie database site, Millie was also the most-viewed celebrity page of 2016. Before long, she seemed to be everywhere: chatting with Ellen Degeneres, dancing with fellow castmates at the Emmys, rapping on *The Tonight Show with Jimmy Fallon*, hamming it up on red carpets. Meanwhile, her Instagram following exploded to over 18 million followers.

Monster/Hero

Why did Millie's performance as Eleven resonate so much? There is no question part of it has to do with her superhero-like role. She is part of a wave of iconic female action heroes in film and television over the past decade, from Katniss Everdeen (played by

Jennifer Lawrence) in *Hunger Games*, to Rey (played by Daisy Ridley) in *Star Wars*, to Wonder Woman (played by Gal Gadot), to Daenerys Targaryen in *Game of Thrones* (played by Emilia Clarke). Even *Ghostbusters* was remade with an all-female cast. Like these women, Eleven is often praised as a strong, fierce powerhouse. We see her break bad guys, deliver vengeance to bullies, flip vans, kill Demogorgons, save the world.

Yet part of what makes Eleven an interesting character is also her fragility and vulnerability. It is the moment we see her crying at night in the makeshift basement bed Mike makes for her; it is the moment she stares at her reflection in the lake, screaming out her pent-up pain; it is her visceral terror after being submerged in the sensory deprivation pool in the gym at Hawkins Middle School, which reminds her of her scariest memories from Hawkins Lab.

Eleven is a survivor. But as we learn through her frequent flashbacks, she hasn't forgotten her past trauma. She carries her history with her.

This is also the genius of Millie Bobby Brown's performance: how she is able to communicate this sense of trauma and abandonment and tenderness in one scene, and then in another, with a simple stare and bow of the head, a goosebump-eliciting strength and power.

Throughout the show, Eleven wrestles with different dimensions of her identity. At times, she acts out of compassion, assistance, and self-sacrifice; at times out of jealousy, anger, and revenge. In Season 1, Chapter 6 ("The Monster") she refers to herself as a monster. She feels responsible for the consequences of her powers, which can at times be wielded, intentionally or not, for destructive ends. She knows she has a dark side. That side typically emerges when she is pushed past her breaking point. In Season 1, Chapter 3 ("Holly, Jolly"), for example, after she refuses to kill a cat in Hawkins Lab, she is dragged to a solitary confinement cell. As the door is about to shut, however, she lowers her head, and slams one guard into the wall, and snaps the other one's neck.

While that act may be justified as self-defense, El's powers are used at times without the same discretion or necessity. In Season 1, Chapter 4 ("The Body"), when she sees Lucas fighting with Mike, for instance, she throws him to the ground so hard it knocks him out, surprising even herself. In Season 2, Chapter 3 ("The Pollywog"), when she sees Max getting friendly with Mike, she causes her to trip and fall off her skateboard.

Eleven occasionally even uses her powers against those with whom she is closest. In Chapter 4 ("Will the Wise"), she has an epic, drag-out fight with Chief Hopper, with whom she is living, culminating in a psychic tantrum that leaves the cabin in shambles and Eleven alone and sobbing on her bedroom floor. Producer Shawn Levy described it as a "clash of the titans." The raw energy in the scene, as she and Hopper exchange threats and insults, is a great example of why Millie has received such acclaim as a young actress. She makes you feel every ounce of the whirlwind of emotions she is experiencing. But it also reveals the struggle she faces in harnessing her powers and figuring out when and how they should be used.

Eleven's character evolves in interesting ways over the first two seasons. In Season 1, as the Duffer Brothers have explained, she is a kind of fish out of water. She has never experienced friends, school, home, Eggos. Moreover, she hasn't tested her powers outside Hawkins Lab. Everything, therefore, is new and strange.

A big part of Season 1 is also establishing her origin story, which we get in fragments. We learn that she is called Eleven (011 is tattooed on her wrist) because she was a test subject at Hawkins Lab; we learn that she was kidnapped from her real mother, Terry Ives, at birth; we learn that she was raised by Dr. Brenner (whom she refers to as Papa), who acts as a sort of stage-parent, exploiting her gifts as part of a larger, government-funded project to use the mind as a geopolitical weapon.

We learn that in her culminating "test" she was lowered into a sensory deprivation tank, which allowed her to reach a psychic state visualized as "The Void." "Today is a very special day," Dr. Brenner tells her. "Do you know why?" El shakes her head no. "Because today," Brenner declares, "we make history."

Making history, however, comes at a cost. In the Void, a wide-eyed El comes across a strange creature. When she approaches and touches it, it turns and shrieks at her, sending El into a fit of terror. Rather than protect her from the creature, Brenner, intrigued by the prospect of an extra-dimensional discovery, arranges for her to go back down into the sensory deprivation tank and return to the Void, promising her she won't be hurt. Brenner, of course, is wrong. This time she inadvertently opens a portal to a dangerous alternate dimension: the Upside Down.

In this way, Eleven is both implicated in the terror that descends on Hawkins—and its only hope for survival.

Sacrifice

Of course, none of this is known when the boys discover El in the woods while looking for Will in Season 1, Chapter 1 ("The Vanishing of Will Byers"). They simply see a frightened child with a shaved head in a hospital gown. When they bring her back to Mike's house, they have no idea what to make of her. Lucas thinks she's crazy. Dustin, at least initially, agrees. Mike is the only one who seems to intuitively understand her. Their relationship, captured with remarkable on-screen chemistry, has been cited by many critics and fans alike as one of the highlights of the show.

Trapped for so long in the cold, sterile confines of Hawkins Laboratory, Mike offers her warmth and acceptance. He provides refuge. There is something genuinely beautiful and touching about their interactions in Season 1. Through her eyes and her expressions, one can feel how much Mike's simple acts of kindness mean to Eleven. She tries to return that kindness in a number of ways, including using her powers to help him find Will. For example, in Chapter 4 ("The Body"), she channels Will on the walkie talkie. Eleven's face as she watches Mike's elation at hearing Will perfectly captures the purity and authenticity of their friendship. It is also yet another example of the subtle brilliance of Millie Bobby Brown's performance.

Ultimately, Eleven wins over the trust of the other boys—not only by wowing them with her telekinetic powers, but also by proving she is a true friend and ally. In Chapter 6 ("The Monster"), after she helps them escape the agents from Hawkins Lab, Lucas apologizes in the junkyard for dismissing and excluding her. "I was wrong," he says, extending his hand. "I'm sorry." From that point on, she is part of the group.

In the final few episodes of Season 1, El proves instrumental in locating Barb and Will and protecting her new friends from a host of encroaching dangers. This takes tremendous courage. In Chapter 6 ("The Monster") , when she goes into the sensory deprivation pool, she is, in essence, facing one of her worst fears. The last time she went in the water, in the Lab, she made contact with the extra-dimensional creature they later refer to as the demogorgon and accidentally opened the gate to the Upside Down. But now she willingly goes back to find Barb and Will, discovering that the former is dead, and the latter is still alive—barely.

In Chapter 8 ("The Upside Down"), meanwhile, it seems she has expended every last ounce of energy shielding her friends from the agents from Hawkins lab. But somehow, in the final showdown with the Demogorgon, she summons the strength to stand and walk straight toward the creature that once horrified her. She looks back at her friends one final time and says, "Goodbye, Mike," before reaching out her hand toward the demogorgon, transfusing her power until the creature—and she—turn to ashes.

Her friends—and the audience—initially assume she is dead: that she has sacrificed her life to save the people she has come to love. This, indeed, was the plan in the original script. The Duffers initially conceived *Stranger Things* as a one-season show. Having Eleven sacrifice herself to save her friends—and Hawkins—packed the biggest punch.

Yet due to the success of the show, Netflix wanted another season, and there was no way they were doing it without Millie's iconic character. The Duffers, then, were forced to figure out a different ending: one in which she could perform the heroic, sacrificial act, but at least hint to the audience that she would be back. That was accomplished by having Hopper leave food for her out in the woods, which, of course, included Eggo waffles.

Transformation

How does Eleven return after the heroic act in which she seemingly vanished into ashes at the end of Season 1? It turns out she was transported into the Upside Down. Down the dark, vine-covered hall she sees a glowing portal—the same portal in which the Demogorgon emerged in Hawkins Middle School. Eleven's emergence through the gooey aperture in the wall is like a birth—or rebirth—which is significant given the journey she subsequently embarks on.

El's character arc for the second season is different than the first. As the Duffers explain: "What we got excited about early on is this idea of Eleven as a fish out of water adjusting to a new world in season one, and now it's more about Eleven growing up outside of the lab. How does she deal with the trauma of what happened to her, just as everyone else has been dealing with their trauma? And does she use that experience for good or for bad?...It allowed us to explore relationships we wouldn't have been allowed to explore otherwise."

Primary among those new relationships is with Chief Hopper. Like Season 1, we don't see Eleven until the end of the first episode. This time, however, she is not a frightened girl in the woods; she is living with Hopper in a remote cabin. There they have established certain routines, rituals, and rules, which boil down to: not taking risks and not being stupid. This essentially means that Eleven must remain trapped in the cabin, with curtains drawn and doors locked, where she quickly begins to feel isolated, bored, and restless.

Just as the dynamic between El and Mike was one of the highlights of Season 1, the dynamic between El and Hopper is undoubtedly one of the best things about Season 2. Millie Bobby Brown described their on-screen chemistry as "electric." "I think it was really good for Millie to be around an actor like [David Harbour]," said Matt Duffer, "an actor who's really going to challenge her to do stuff she's not expecting." Millie concurred. "He brought so much energy and greatness into a scene," she said, "that I would just get to kind of bounce off of it." The pairing not only resonated because of great talent and chemistry, but also because it captured a familiar parent-child dynamic, at times warm and tender, and at times tense and combative. He wants to protect and shield her from danger; she wants more freedom and independence.

Eventually, El is fed up with spending the majority of her days alone and without purpose, and breaks her agreement with Hopper about leaving the cabin. She first seeks out Mike at school, but ends up not talking to him after finding him with Max. Next she seeks out her mother, whom she learns of through files in a storage box hidden beneath the cabin floor. While her mother is a shell of her former self, El is able to communicate with her in the Void and fill in more gaps about her past. She learns how she was taken from her mother at birth, how her mother was tortured when attempting to rescue her, and, significantly, how she was not alone in the "rainbow room" — she had a sister.

This sets up Chapter 7 ("The Lost Sister"), the only episode to take place outside of Hawkins — and perhaps the most polarizing episode of the first two seasons. In spite of the criticism, the Duffers felt the episode was necessary in particular for Eleven's evolution, akin to Luke Skywalker going to Dagobah, where he meets and is trained by Yoda. "[We] wanted Eleven to have her own journey and have this journey of self-discovery," explained Matt Duffer. "...Eleven is trying to figure out where she belongs in this world. She doesn't belong with the boys because she can't exist with them without putting them in danger. Her existence with Hopper, which seemed promising at first — this is a guy she believed would protect her and help her find her way back in the world — is seemingly failing. She's really at a loss. She goes to her mother, but she's not there, basically. So that's not a home for her. Basically, it's her looking for a home."

What she finds, however, is not a home as much as a revelation about herself. In Kali, Eleven finds someone, finally, who understands the pain and trauma of her past. Like El, Kali was a test subject at Hawkins Lab, assigned the number "008," which, like El, is tattooed on her wrist. In Kali, Eleven also finds someone who has a supernatural gift — in Kali's case, the ability to create illusions. Kali encourages El to not think of herself as a freak or a monster, or be ashamed of her abilities, but to use them. Kali tells El that finding her has finally made her "feel whole"; El feels the same.

El's physical metamorphosis — from small-town flannel and overalls, to slicked back hair, black jacket, and eyeliner (known as "Punk Eleven") — symbolizes her character's transformation and newfound allegiance to Kali's group of injured outsiders. Yet as the episode progresses, it becomes clear that their life experiences since leaving the lab—and personalities—are not exactly the same. Kali wants El to develop her power by channeling her pain and rage. El is not entirely unfamiliar with this method and in some ways finds it liberating and cathartic. But when she is asked to murder a man from Hawkins Lab responsible for her mother's condition, she can't bring herself to do it. She sees a photo of the man's daughters and suddenly halts. When Kali pulls out a gun to do the job herself, El throws the gun out the window.

The incident causes a fissure in their relationship, but also prompts an epiphany for El. She realizes this is not the life she wants and that her home is in Hawkins—with Mike and Hopper and the rest of the gang. They're the ones who first took her in and cared for her when she was lost and abandoned. And they are the ones who now need her the most—not for individual acts of revenge or retribution, but for defense against a much larger and more imminent threat.

In a vision created by Kali in the warehouse, Papa (Brenner) visits Eleven and warns her: "You have to confront your pain. You have a wound, Eleven. A terrible wound. And it's festering. Do you remember what that means? Festering. It means a rot. And it will grow and spread. And eventually, it will kill you." Kali wants El to recognize the need to face her demons and avenger her mother. Instead, however, it further solidifies El's decision to leave her sister and return to Hawkins.

Punk Eleven's entrance through the Byers' door at the end of Chapter 8 is a beautifully orchestrated, goosebumps moment. We see her white sneakers, her rolled jeans. Then we see the stunned reaction of Hopper, Mike, and the rest of the group. And finally, the full reveal of the new Eleven, who has returned from her quest, now wiser and stronger, and whose bloody nose indicates that she has, once again, saved their lives—this time from the surrounding demodogs.

In the final chapter of Season 2, El teams up with Hopper again. They apologize for their mistakes—in fact, Hopper even concedes that her new, MTV punk look is pretty "bitchin.'" El, of course, also reunites with Mike—first, at the house, and later at the Snowball Dance—another goosebumps moment that highlights El's softer side. It is these reunions with the people she cares about most that actually heal the wound and fill the void that ignited her quest in the first place.

Yet as in Season 1, it takes a miraculous effort to protect the people she loves from being destroyed. This time, she and Hopper descend into the basement of Hawkins Lab, where the once small portal has now become an enormous, volcanic opening. There, in the depths of the cavernous threshold, Hopper picks off demodogs with his shotgun as El begins to focus her mind on fusing the string-like tissues of the Gate. Closing the Gate demands everything El can summon. She reaches both hands forward, recalling Kali's advice to channel her pain and rage, screaming as she looks into the fiery furnace.

The visual of El, bleeding from both nostrils, arms outstretched, elevated off the ground, sparks flying, as the Gate slowly begins to weld, is breathtaking and powerful. It not only demanded everything of her character, but also of her as an actress. Millie remembers being nauseous and utterly exhausted after finishing the scene.

When the Gate is finally sealed, she collapses into Hopper's arms. They hold onto each other as the elevator ascends back up through the ashes toward the light.

We Can Be Heroes

For what she represents—her bravery, eccentricity, authenticity, and power—Eleven has become a hero to girls and boys alike all over the world. In 2018, *Time* included Millie Bobby Brown on its list of 100 Most Influential People in the world. She was the youngest person ever to receive the recognition.

For Brown, that is what has been among the most fulfilling aspects of playing the role. "I didn't think Eleven would be that popular," she acknowledged. "I thought she would just be the sidekick...but Eleven I think resonates because she is different. She's an outcast, she's a freak, and that is why people relate to her."

In an acceptance speech at the 2017 Critics Choice Awards, David Harbour reflected on his intertwined odyssey with Eleven (Millie Bobby Brown). "In *Stranger Things* this season," he said,

> Hopper spends the majority of the fall of '84 holed up in a cabin with a maturing young woman, desperately, stumblingly trying to care for her as her ever-adapting, evolving needs slip through his unsophisticated fingers, his rigid beliefs, his fear that the world isn't ready. The world isn't ready for the secret, inherent power she has inside her. She's feral, he her guardian. The cabin is safe, comforting, and it's dangerous out there, and yet she leaves.

He continues:

> When re-connected with her sister she is lit aflame and carries this fire, this light back to Hawkins and re-unites with Hopper and now he himself must be guided by the North Star of her powerful coming to being. Because he loves her and because he needs her. She is the key to resurrecting life, cleansing the infection, closing the rift.

Harbour closed his remarks by thanking "the gifted and incomparable Millie Bobby Brown" for being his "sparring partner" and inspiration, as well as the "incandescent" Winona Ryder for being his light. The speech went viral and drove home the importance of women to the show.

After the first season, some critics argued that *Stranger Things* had a "limited view on women." They pointed to the lack of attention paid to Barb's disappearance compared to Will, or the fact that Joyce's character seems to revolve entirely around her son, as indicative of the show's shortcomings. Asked about this critique after Season 1, Matt Duffer countered that he believed each of the major female characters had a "strong drive" and dynamic identity that would only grow and deepen in Season 2.

We certainly see this with Eleven. She is featured at the center of the cover art for the show for a reason—she is its central hero.

Joseph Campbell famously defined the hero's journey as a universal, archetypal quest in which the individual must pass through a number of thresholds to grow or achieve further enlightenment.

There are a variety of iterations of those thresholds, but generally, they go something like this: First, the hero must accept or respond to the call of adventure (often, this is when one is introduced to a mentor or guide); second, the hero meets some kind of resistance; third, the hero faces greater challenges or obstacles; fourth, there is some kind of supreme, culminating crisis; fifth, the hero is transformed or reborn; sixth, they must synthesize or process the meaning of their journey and transformation; and seventh, they must return and in some way use the new knowledge or power they have gained to help their fellow beings. It is easy to see how closely Eleven's journey in *Stranger Things* follows this arc.

But it is not just Eleven who embarks on a hero's journey. While she is the show's central hero, each character is developed enough to have their own identity, abilities, and purpose. This, indeed, is the concept of "the Party" from Dungeons & Dragons.

Everyone has a role to play. We see these roles unfold at the end of Season 2 like a carefully conducted orchestra.

Hopper nearly kills himself navigating the toxic underground tunnels that lead to the Upside Down and later serves as Eleven's right-hand man as she closes the Gate. Bob sacrifices his life to get the power back on in Hawkins Lab. Steve looks after the kids (taking a beating in the process). Dustin prevents Dart from killing his friends. Lucas refuses to be intimidated by Billy. Max puts an end to her brother's violent rampage. Joyce and Mike help Will exorcise the Mind Flayer. And Nancy and Jonathan expose Hawkins Lab and vindicate Barb.

Everyone contributes and every contribution is crucial to the success of the mission. That's the beauty of the show. Sure, it features extraterrestrial monsters and supernatural concepts, but its central appeal is its characters. It is the characters that make us keep watching. It is the characters that make the '80s come to life with such vitality. It is the characters who feel so authentic and familiar that we believe in their quest. It is the characters who make the Bowie lyrics ring true:

> *Oh, we can beat them, forever and ever*
> *Then we could be heroes just for one day*

Notes

_____

Introduction

1   "While Netflix is...": John Koblin, "New Netflix Ratings
     Confirm 'Stranger Things' Is a Hit," *New York Times*, November
     2, 2017.

2   "That mont the *New York Times*...": Neil Genzlinger, "Review:
     With 'Stranger Things,' Netflix Delivers an Eerie Nostalgia Fix,"
     New York Times, July 14, 2016.

3   "By Season 2...": Brian Barrett, "How Netflix Made 'Stranger
     Things' a Global Phenomenon," *Wired*, October 23, 2017.

4   "If I have one goal...": "Next Gen 2014: Hollywood's New
     Class," *The Hollywood Reporter*, November 4, 2014.

5   "Before the meeting...": Geoff Berkshire, "'Stranger Things':
     Shawn Levy on Directing Winona Ryder, Netflix's Viral Model,"
     Variety, July 22, 2016.

6   "In the movie business...": Jack Giroux, "Interview: 'Stranger
     Things' Producers on Influences, Marketing, the Possibility of
     Future Seasons and More," *Film*, July 21, 2016.

7   "When we sold this...": Geoff Berkshire, "'Stranger Things':
     Shawn Levy on Directing Winona Ryder, Netflix's Viral Model,"
     Variety, July 22, 2016.

8   "We're an enigma..": Anna Garvey, "The Oregon Trail
     Generation: Life Before and After Mainstream Tech." *Social
     Media Week*. April 21, 2015.

9   "If you can distinctly…": *Ibid.*

10   "I don't remember the 1980s…": David Sirota, *Back To Our Future: How the 1980s Explain the World We Live in Now--Our Culture, Our Politics, Our Everything* (New York: Ballantine Books, 2011), p. xiii.

11   "Patched together a common dialect…": *Ibid.*

12   "In [our] household…": *Ibid.*

13   "Pay homage to all the things…": Kory Grow, "'Stranger Things': How Two Brothers Created Summer TV's Biggest Hit," *Rolling Stone*, August 3, 2017.

14   "Sometimes I see people…": Melissa Leon, "Inside 'Stranger Things': The Duffer Bros. On How They Made the TV Hit of the Summer," *The Daily Beast*, August 7, 2016.

15   "These are the movies…": Esther Zuckerman, "The Duffers Want Some Scares With their Spielberg," *The A.V. Club*, July 13, 2016.

16   "Our goal [was] to make…": Matt Grobar, "'Stranger Things' Cinematographer Tim Ives On Shooting the Upside Down," *Deadline*, August 26, 2017.

17   "He was known…": The Duffer Brothers, "Stranger Things premiere episode: The Duffer Brothers introduce their new Netflix series," *Entertainment Weekly*, July 15, 2016.

18   "As soon as we heard…": The Duffer Brothers, "Stranger Things episode 5: The Duffer Brothers explain the show's soundtrack," *Entertainment Weekly*, July 19, 2016.

19   For *Stranger Things*, the Duffers…": *Ibid.*

20   "The Duffers loved its vibe…": Hanh Nguyen, "'Stranger Things' Composers Interview: Duo Discusses Soundtrack, That Haunting Theme Song and More," *IndieWire*, August 10, 2016.

Chapter 1: Stephen King

1   "I mean that in a good way…": Stephen King (Twitter), "Watching STRANGER THINGS is looking watching Steve King's Greatest Hits. I mean that in a good way," July 17, 2016. 10:29am.

2   "Growing up he was…": Chris Gardner, "Stephen King Is Email Buddies With the 'Stranger Things' Creators," The Hollywood

Reporter, September 28, 2017.

3   "According to *Publisher Weekly*…": Tony Magistrale, *Stephen King: America's Storyteller* (Santa Barbara: Praeger, 2010), p. 11.

4   "In a *Time* cover story…": Stefan Kanfer, "King of Horror," *Time*, October 6, 1986.

5   "Another low in the shocking process…": Harold Bloom, "Dumbing Down American Readers," *Boston.com*, September 24, 2003.

6   "In his book, *Nightmare*…": Mark Edmundson, *Nightmare on Main Street: Angels, Sadomasochism, and the Culture of Gothic* (Cambridge: Harvard University Press, 1999).

7   "What the Beatles were…": Tony Magistrale, *Stephen King: America's Storyteller* (Santa Barbara: Praeger, 2010), p. 12.

8   "I thought it was true…": Mike Scott, "Stephen King picks his favorite Stephen King movies," *The Times-Picayune*, November 4, 2014.

9   "Ross Duffer describes…": Jen Chaney, "Stranger Things' Duffer Brothers on '80s Cinema, Fighting Over Kid Actors, and How They Cast Winona Ryder," Vulture, July 15, 2016.

10   "We love that story…": The Duffer Brothers, "*Stranger Things* episode 4: The Duffer Brothers inspired by Stephen King," *Entertainment Weekly*, July 18, 2016.

11   "Will Wheaton, who played Gordie…": Meriah Doty, "Wil Wheaton on Why 'Stranger Things' Could Be This Generation's 'Stand By Me,'" *The Wrap*, July 27, 2016.

12   "It's what makes something…": *Ibid.*

13   "It's the big one…": Daniel Fienberg, "The Duffer Brothers Talk 'Stranger Things' Influences, 'It' Dreams and Netflix Phase 2," *The Hollywood Reporter*, August 1, 2016.

14   "After Seaason 2 premiered…": Bob Bradley, "The Truth Behind The Creepy Connection Between 'It' And 'Stranger Things,'" *Huffington Post*, November 7, 2017.

15   "It was a real problem…": Jeff Chaney, "The Duffer Brothers Recap *Stranger Things 2*, 'Chapter Three: The Pollywog,'" *Vulture*, November 1, 2017.

16   "Stephen King exists…": *Ibid.*

17   "*Carrie* is largely about…": Stephen King, *Danse Macabre* (New York: Gallery Books, 2010), p. 180.

18   "After watching Season 1…": Stephen King (Twitter),
        "STRANGER THINGS is pure fun. A+. Don't miss it. Winona
        Ryder shines," July 17, 2016. 9:28pm.

19   "Likewise, after watching the second season…": Stephen King
        (Twitter), "STRANGER THINGS 2: Ladies and gentlemen,
        that's how you do it: no bullshit, balls to the wall
        entertainment. Straight up," November 8, 2017. 9:21pm.

20   "He's amazing…": Daniel Fienberg, "The Duffer Brothers Talk
        'Stranger Things' Influences, 'It' Dreams and Netflix Phase 2,"
        The Hollywood Reporter, August 1, 2016.

Chapter 2: Spielberg

1   "I don't know how Stephen King…": Anthony Breznican, "The
        untold story of Stephen King and Steven Spielberg's (almost)
        collaborations," *Entertainment Weekly*, April 5, 2018.

2   "What Spielberg did in the '80s…": Rebecca Nicholson, "The
        Duffer Brothers: 'Could we do what Spielberg did in the '80s
        and elevate it?" *The Guardian*, October 14, 2017.

3   "Director of Photography Tim Ives…": Ashley Rodriguez,
        "Watch: The opening scene of "Stranger Things" owes
        everything to "E.T.," *Quartz*, October 27, 2017.

4   "We held our breath…": The Duffer Brothers, "Stranger Things
        premiere episode: The Duffer Brothers introduce their new
        Netflix series," *Entertainment Weekly*, July 15, 2016.

5   "In E.T., Elliot…": Ashley Rodriguez, "Watch: The opening
        scene of "Stranger Things" owes everything to "E.T.," *Quartz*,
        October 27, 2017.

6   "There was a shot…": *Ibid*.

7   "Becomes the quintessential stranger…": The Duffer Brothers,
        " *Stranger Things* episode 2: The Duffer Brothers on finding
        their Eleven," *Entertainment Weekly*, July 16, 2016.

8   "Eleven isn't a normal girl…": *Ibid*.

9   "We liked Montauk…": Daniel Fienberg, "The Duffer Brothers
        Talk 'Stranger Things' Influences, 'It' Dreams and Netflix Phase
        2," *The Hollywood Reporter*, August 1, 2016.

10   "An interdimensional being…": Jefferson Grubbs, "Is The
        'Stranger Things' Monster An Alien? The Nature Of This Beast

Isn't Quite So Straightforward," *Bustle*, July 25, 2016.

11   "When I come into our consensus reality...": Kelly Lawler, "How the shark from 'Jaws' inspired the 'Stranger Things' Monster," *USA Today*, August 24, 2016.

12   "A perfect eating machine...": *Ibid*.

13   "We knew [Wynona Ryder]...": Leah Thomas, "Winona Ryder's Casting In 'Stranger Things' Wasn't An '80s Reference, But She Did Inspire One Of The Show's Best Nods," *Bustle*, August 23, 2016.

14   "Everyone thinks he's making a mountain...": Rebecca Nicholson, "The Duffer Brothers: 'Could we do what Spielberg did in the '80s and elevate it?" *The Guardian*, October 14, 2017.

15   "I love that it gets...": Chris Tilly, "6 Things The 'Stranger Things' Writers Told Us About Season 2," *IGN*, August 23, 2016.

16   "That's the whole bedroomd dance...": Rachel Paige, "The Duffer Brothers want you to know "Stranger Things" Season 2 is full of "Indiana Jones" references," *Hello Giggles*, October 27, 2017.

17   "That's exactly like Short Round...": Daniel, D'Addario, "Stories From the Set of *Stranger Things*, the TV Escape We Need Right Now," *Time*, October 17, 2017.

18   "Andrew Stanton, who directed...": Rachel Paige, "The Duffer Brothers want you to know "Stranger Things" Season 2 is full of "Indiana Jones" references," *Hello Giggles*, October 27, 2017.

19   "Aside from Will being possessed...": Jen Chaney, "The Duffer Brothers Recap *Stranger Things 2*, 'Chapter Three: The Pollywog,'" *Vulture*, November 1, 2017.

20   "That Sean Astin soft-spoken...": Dana Getz, "This 'Goonies' Reference In 'Stranger Things' Season 2 Is A Shameless Tribute To One The Show's Biggest Inspirations," *Bustle*, October 30, 2017.

21   "Sean loved [the reference]...": *Ibid*.

22   "According to producer Shawn Levy...": Yohana Desta, "*Stranger Things*: Winona Ryder Cried for 10 Hours During the Christmas Lights Scene," *Vanity Fair*, June 23, 2017.

23   "While producer Steven Spielberg hasn't...": *Ibid*.

24   "We don't talk about the fact...": *Ibid*.

Chapter 3: '80s Movies

1   "John Carpenter mashed up with E.T....": Rebecca Nicholson, "The Duffer Brothers: 'Could we do what Spielberg did in the '80s and elevate it?" *The Guardian*, October 14, 2017.

2   "I'm not an accomplished...": David Konow, "The Making of John Carpenter's Halloween," *Consequence of Sound*, October 31, 2017.

3   "We wanted an all-electronic...": Esther Zuckerman, "The *Stranger Things* creators want some scares with their Spielberg," *AV Club*, July 13, 2016.

4   "We shot on a digital camera...": *Ibid*.

5   "Our approach to lensing...": Matt Grobar, "'Stranger Things' Cinematographer Tim Ives On Shooting The Upside Down," *Deadline*, August 26, 2017.

6   "Like so many filmmakers...": The Duffer Brothers, "*Stranger Things* episode 6: How the Duffer Brothers created the monster," *Entertainment Weekly*, July 20, 2016.

7   "The first time we saw...": *Ibid*.

8   "We looked a lot...": Matthew Jacobs, "'Stranger Things' Creators Mourn Barb, Geek Out Over The Millennium Falcon And Tease Season 2," *Huffington Post*, July 28, 2017.

9   "I love that people argue...": Josh Wigler, "'Stranger Things': How 'Aliens' Influenced Season 2," *The Hollywood Reporter*, November 9, 2017.

10   "Paul Reiser described...": Maria Elena Fernandez, "Paul Reiser on *Stranger Things 2, Aliens*, and Saying Good-bye to *Red Oaks*," *Vulture*, October 28, 2017.

11   "While everyone else runs...": Abraham Reissman, "Paul Reiser in *Stranger Things* Is Stunt Casting at Its Best," *Vulture*, October 31, 2017.

12   "*Stranger Things* is doing...": *Ibid*.

13   "It's funny...": Matthew Jacobs, "'Stranger Things' Creators Mourn Barb, Geek Out Over The Millennium Falcon And Tease Season 2," *Huffington Post*, July 28, 2017.

14   "Talked a lot about Empire Strikes Back...": Tim Stack, "How that polarizing *Stranger Things 2* episode was inspired by *Star*

Wars," *Entertainment Weekly,* November 1, 2017.

15   "I took everything from Luke…": *Ibid.*

16   "We had this very nervous speech…": Jen Chaney, "The Duffer Brothers Recap *Stranger Things 2*, 'Chapter Two: Trick or Treat, Freak,'" *Vulture,* October 31, 2017.

17   "These kids would be…" *Ibid.*

Chapter 4: '80s Music

1   *"Rolling Stone* included…": "500 Greatest Songs of All Time," *Rolling Stone,* April 7, 2011.

2   "For us, we didn't Tarantino it…": Andrew Gruttadaro, "How the Duffer Brothers Picked the Perfect Music for 'Stranger Things,'" *Complex,* August 2, 2016.

3   "With his photography…": Noah Yoo. "Inside the Spellbinding Sound of 'Stranger Things,'" *Pitchfork,* August 16, 2016.

4   "Kind of a rule we had…": Andrew Gruttadaro, "How the Duffer Brothers Picked the Perfect Music for 'Stranger Things,'" *Complex,* August 2, 2016.

5   "There's not been a trailer…": Jesse Kinos-Goodin, "Stranger Things producer says cost of 'Thriller' was stratospheric, but worth it," *CBC,* August 21, 2017.

6   "Just weeks before Comic-con…": *Ibid.*

7   "The [Duffer] brothers and I…": Cheryl Eddy, *"Stranger Things* Producer Shawn Levy Had to Move Mountains to Get the Rights to 'Thriller,'" *io9,* July 31, 2017.

8   "We always wanted…": Jen Chaney, "The Duffer Brothers Recap *Stranger Things 2* Finale, 'Chapter 9: The Gate,'" *Vulture,* November 10, 2017.

Chapter 5: Childhood

1   "Today, that number…": Jessica Gross and Hanna Rosin, "The Shortening Leash," *Slate,* August 6, 2014.

2   "I think it was the freedom…": Jen Chaney, *"Stranger Things'* Millie Bobby Brown on Playing Eleven, Her Love-Hate Relationship With Scary Movies, and Acting Without Speaking," *Vulture,* July 18, 2016.

3   "We grew up without...": Esther Zuckerman, "The 'Stranger Things' creators want some scares with their Spielberg," *AV Club*, July 13, 2016.

4   "Bikes allow the kids...": Glen Weldon, "Kids On Bikes: The Sci-Fi Nostalgia Of 'Stranger Things', 'Paper Girls' & 'Super 8,'" *NPR*, July 27, 2016.

5   "Mike's bike is actually...": Tim Moynihan, "The Stories Behind 'Stranger Things' Retro '80s Props," *Wired*, July 27, 2016.

6   "The Duffer Brothers told...": The Duffer Brothers, "Stranger Things: The Duffer Brothers say episode 7 is the 'most fun,'" *Entertainment Weekly*, July 21, 2016.

7   "Lambert was inspired...": Kat Thompson, "Meet Kyle Lambert, the Movie Poster Artist Behind the Now-Iconic Stranger Things Poster," *The Hundreds*, August 17, 2016.

8   "We literally took...": Daniel Feinberg, "The Duffer Brothers Talk 'Stranger Things' Influences, 'It' Dreams and Netflix Phase 2," *The Hollywood Reporter*, August 1, 2016.

9   "Eventually, as kidnapping rang...": Paula Fuss, *Kidnapped: Child Abduction in America* (Cambridge: Harvard University Press, 1999), p. 6.

10   "Paradoxically, that is...": *Ibid.* p. 7.

11   "Divorce rates nearly doubled...": W. Bradford Wilcox, "The Evolution of Divorce," *National Affairs* 35 (Fall 2009).

12   "Yes, they seem like...": Matthew Jacobs, "'Stranger Things' Creators Mourn Barb, Geek Out Over The Millennium Falcon And Tease Season 2," *Huffington Post*, July 28, 2016.

Chapter 6: The Reagan Era

1   "Mired in a deep recession...": Frank Newport, Jeffrey M. Jones, and Lydia Saad, "Ronald Reagan From the People's Perspective: A Gallup Poll Review," *Gallup*, June 7, 2004.

2   "You've got steam...": Jen Chaney, "The Duffer Brothers Recap *Stranger Things 2*, 'Chapter Seven: The Lost Sister,'" *Vulture*, November 7, 2017.

3   "Ronald Reagan described...": Troy Gil, *Morning in America: How Ronald Reagan Invented the 1980s* (New Jersey: Princeton

University Press, 2005).

4   "Rather, it was the result...": James Baldwin, *The Evidence of Things Not Seen* (New York: Holt, 1995), p. 74.

5   "Even President Reagan...": Hannah McBride, "The TV Movie That Terrified America," *The Outline*, July 17, 2017.

6   "Whether it was MKUltra...": Esther Zuckerman, "The 'Stranger Things' creators want some scares with their Spielberg," *AV Club*, July 13, 2016.

7   "In his Inaugural Address...": Ronald Reagan, Inaugural Address, January 20, 1981. http://www.presidency.ucsb.edu/ws/?pid=43130

8   "Most people are at least...": John Napier Tye, "Meet Executive Order 12333: The Reagan rule that lets the NSA spy on Americans," *Washington Post*, July 18, 2014.

9   "Journalist David Sirota...": David Sirota, *Back To Our Future: How the 1980s Explain the World We Live in Now--Our Culture, Our Politics, Our Everything* (New York: Ballantine Books, 2011), p. xvii.

Chapter 7: Playing Games

1   "Homoerotic *Top Gun* volleyball vibe...": E. Alex Jung, "*Stranger Things*' Joe Keery Agrees That Steve's Jeans Were Very Tight," *Vulture*, October 30, 2017.

2   "These kids were big D&D nerds...": Josh Oakley, "Interview: The Duffer Brothers & Shawn Levy of 'Stranger Things,'" *cutprintfilm*, August 3, 2016.

3   "Such demonic characters...": "The Great Dungeons & Dragons Panic," *BBC*, April 11, 2014.

4   "Conservative Christian groups...": *Ibid*.

5   "It has nothing to do with...": Jen Chaney, "The Duffer Brothers Recap *Stranger Things 2*, 'Chapter Eight: The Mind Flayer,'" *Vulture*, November 8, 2017.

6   "We were hoping...": *Ibid*.

7   "A 1982 cover story...": "Gronk! Flash! Zap! Video Games Are Blitzing the World," *Time*, January 18, 1982.

8   "Those machines generated...": Leslie Haddon, "Electronic and Computer Games: The History of an Interactive Medium"

Screen, 22.9 (March 1988), pp. 52–73.

9   *"Pac-Man* was also credited...": *How to Win Video Games* (New York: Pocket Books, 1982), p. 86.

10   "The jingling quarters...": Rian Dundon, "Photos: The golden age of video arcades," *Timeline*, December 17, 2016.

11   "Our production designer...": Jen Chaney, "The Duffer Brothers Recap Stranger Things 2, 'Chapter One: MadMax,'" *Vulture*, October 30, 2017.

12   "The popularity of video games...": Michael Newman, "Children of the '80s Never Fear: Video Games Did Not Ruin Your Life," *Smithsonian*, May 25, 2017.

Chapter 8: Science & Technology

1   "There was interference...": Jen Chaney, "The Duffer Brothers Recap *Stranger Things 2*, 'Chapter Three: The Pollywog,'" *Vulture*, November 1, 2017.

2   "A watershed moment...": Dave Itzkoff, "'Family Guy' Creator Part of 'Cosmos' Update," *New York Times*, August 5, 2011.

3   "I want to say something...": Ronald Reagan, "Explosion of the Space Shuttle Challenger Address to the Nation," January 28, 1986

4   "According to prop master...": Tim Moynihan, "The Stories Behind 'Stranger Things' Retro '80s Props," *Wired*, July 27, 2016.

5   "The first stereo...": Tim Moynihan, "The Stories Behind 'Stranger Things' Retro '80s Props," *Wired*, July 27, 2016.

6   "In Will's room...": *Ibid.*

7   "In fact, Polaroid's head...": Thomas Hobbs, "Polaroid on why the 'Stranger Things effect' is good news for retro brands," *Marketing Week*, October 20, 2017.

8   "Thanks to Stranger Things...": *Ibid.*

9   "The walkie talkies we see...": Tim Moynihan, "The Stories Behind 'Stranger Things' Retro '80s Props," *Wired*, July 27, 2016.

10   "These pieces of technology...": Jessica Conditt, "These pieces of technology drive the story and shape the main characters on a fundamental level," *Engadget*, November 23, 2017.

Chapter 9: Food & Fashion

1 "Yet this was not product placement...": Jessica Wohl, "How Eggos Plays Up Its Moment in the 'Stranger Things' Spotlight," *AdAge*, October 16, 2017.

2 "It was just going to be some food...": Jason Guerrasio, "A crucial scene in the last episode of 'Stranger Things' almost didn't happen," *Business Insider*, August 31, 2016.

3 "*Vulture* decalred her...": Brian Moylan, "In Praise of Barb, the Best Character on *Stranger Things*," *Vulture*, July 25, 2016.

4 "*The Daily Beast* referred to her...": Melissa Leon, "Inside 'Stranger Things': The Duffer Bros. on How They Made the TV Hit of the Summer," *The Daily Beast*, August 7, 2016.

5 "*Vanity Fair*, meawhile...": Laura Bradley, "How the Internet Made Barb from *Stranger Things* Happen," *Vanity Fair*, August 24, 2016.

6 "The whole Barb phenomenon...": Shannon Purser (Twitter), "Barb wasn't supposed to be a big deal and you lovely people made her important. Thank you," August 20, 2016, 4:09 pm.

7 "Barb wasn't supposed to be...": Jessica Barrett, "Shannon Purser: 'The whole Barb phenomenon blew me away,'" *iNews*, August 2, 2017.

8 "It was very easy...": "'Stranger Things' Creators On Barb, Eleven And How Glitter Delayed Production," *NPR*, August 19, 2016.

9 "The Duffer Brothers' biggest focus...": Liz Raftery, "Best Dressed: How *Stranger Things*' Costume Designers Took the Show's Generation Z Stars Back to the '80s," *TV Guide*, October 30, 2017.

10 "We tried lots of clothing...": *Ibid*.

11 "Can I be super real...": Shannon Purser (Twitter), "Can I be super real? Didn't think a girl with my body type could get this far. I'm so thankful and excited. Much love to you all," August 30, 2016, 12:36 pm.

12 "I just think no one casts...": 'Stranger Things' Creators On Barb, Eleven And How Glitter Delayed Production," *NPR*, August 19, 2016.

13   "Her family is upper middle class...": Joe Kucharski, "Stranger Things - Costume Designing 1980s Nostalgia," *Tyranny of Style*, November 15, 2016.

14   "In my head...": Elana Fishman, "How Eleven's Bitchin' 'Stranger Things 2' Makeover Came Together," *Racked*, October 31, 2017.

15   "We wanted her to become...": *Ibid.*

16   "I wanted to infuse...": *Ibid.*

17   "I just love the moment...": *Ibid.*

18   "Willox pulled up all these old photos...": Ibid.

19   "We wanted Eleven to see...": Dee Lockett, "It's Nearly Impossible to Get the Farrah Fawcett Hairspray That Steve Uses in Stranger Things," *Vulture*, November 2, 2017.

20   "For the Duffers...": Joe Kucharski, "Stranger Things - Costume Designing 1980s Nostalgia," *Tyranny of Style*, November 15, 2016.

21   "Every detail makes a difference...": Joe Kucharski, "Stranger Things - Costume Designing 1980s Nostalgia," *Tyranny of Style*, November 15, 2016.

Chapter 10: The Outsiders

1   "It was really bad...": "Who Was Ryan White?" HRSA. https://hab.hrsa.gov/about-ryan-white-hivaids-program/who-was-ryan-white

2   "The Duffers acknowledged that Billy...": Jen Chaney, "The Duffer Brothers Recap *Stranger Things 2*, 'Chapter 4: Will the Wise,'" *Vulture*, November 2, 2017.

3   "Lucas's relationship with Max...": *Ibid.*

4   "*Vice* declared his character's evolution...": Jamie Clifton, "The 'Stranger Things' Transformation No One Saw Coming," *Vice*, October 30, 2017

5   "A new fan favorite...": Laura Bradley, "Stranger Things: Why Steve Harrington Should Be Your New Fan Favorite," *Vanity Fair*, October 28, 2017.

6   "That's probably one of my favorite...": E. Alex Jung, "*Stranger Things*' Joe Keery Agrees That Steve's Jeans Were Very Tight," *Vulture*, October 30, 2017.

Chapter 11: A Hero's Journey

1   "Played by Millie Bobby Brown…": Nick Levine, "A Reddit user has counted how many words Eleven says on 'Stranger Things,'" *NME*, September 24, 2016.

2   "In 1990, cultural critic…": Camille Paglia, "Madonna -- Finally, a Real Feminist," *New York Times*, December 14, 1990.

3   "Badass, female, iconic character…": Nina V. Guno, "'Stranger Things' actress Millie Bobby Brown grateful for her 'badass, female, iconic character,'" *Inquirer*, May 9, 2017.

4   "We had five kids…": Josh Oakley, "Interview: The Duffer Brothers & Shawn Levy of 'Stranger Things,'" *cutprintfilm*, August 3, 2016.

5   "Even when we saw dozens…": *Ibid.*

6   "I've never forgotten it…": Natalie Stone, "Millie Bobby Brown Dishes on Her First-Ever Kiss (with Costar Finn Wolfhard!) — and the *Stranger Things* Prop She Kept," *People*, October 31, 2017.

7   "It was the best decision…": Rose Walano, "Watch 'Stranger Things' Star Millie Bobby Brown Shave Her Head to Play Eleven," *US Weekly*, August 22, 2016.

8   "Child actors, even the great ones…"; The Duffer Brothers, "Stranger Things episode 2: The Duffer Brothers on finding their Eleven," *Entertainment Weekly*, July 16, 2016.

9   "A downright spooky..": Debra Birnbaum, "How 'Stranger Things' Star Millie Bobby Brown Made Eleven 'Iconic' and Catapulted Into Pop Culture," *Variety*, October 5, 2017.

10   "We have yet to give her…": Debra Birnbaum, "How 'Stranger Things' Star Millie Bobby Brown Made Eleven 'Iconic' and Catapulted Into Pop Culture," *Variety*, October 5, 2017.

11   "*Vanity Fair* called her…": Richard Lawson, "Stranger Things Is a Scary, Poignant Piece of 1980s Nostalgia," *Vanity Fair*, July 13, 2016.

12   "The *New Yorker* described her…": Emily Nussbaum, "'Stranger Things' and 'The Get Down,'" *New Yorker*, August 22, 2016.

13   "Meanwhile, when bestselling novelist…": Stephen King (Twitter), "Millie Brown, the girl in INTRUDERS, is terrific. Is

it my imagination, or are child actors a lot better than they used to be?" September 28, 2016, 8:54 am.

14   "According to clothing retailer…": Kelly Agnew, "11 Signs That Everyone's Dressing As A Stranger Things Character This Halloween," Lyst, https://www.lyst.com/articles/stranger-things-halloween-costume-ideas/

15   "According to IMBD…": Brianna Wiest, "Millie Bobby Brown Is IMBD's Biggest Breakout Star of 2016," *Teen Vogue*, December 8, 2016.

16   "Producer Shawn Levy described…": Shawn Levy (Twitter), "Between takes while shooting our psychic tantrum scene. A clash of Titans. @milliebbrown @DavidKHarbour #StrangerThings2," October 27, 2017, 10:51 pm.

17   "What we got excited about…": Josh Wigler, "'Stranger Things' Creators Break Down Season 2's Eleven Story," *The Hollywood Reporter*, October 21, 2017.

18   "Millie Bobby Brown described…": *Beyond Stranger Things*, Netflix, 27 October 2017.

19   "I think it was really good…": Jen Chaney, "The Duffer Brothers Recap Stranger Things 2, 'Chapter 4: Will the Wise,'" *Vulture*, November 2, 2017.

20   "He brought so much energy…": *Beyond Stranger Things*, Netflix, 27 October 2017.

21   "We wanted Eleven to have…": Jen Chaney, "The Duffer Brothers Recap *Stranger Things 2*, 'Chapter Seven: The Lost Sister,'" Vulture, November 7, 2017.

22   "In 2018, Time included Millie…": http://time.com/collection/most-influential-people-2018/5238181/millie-bobby-brown/; Jamie Spain, "Millie Bobby Brown Is TIME's Youngest 100 Most Influential People Honoree Ever," *People*, April 19, 2018.

23   "I didn't think Eleven…": Joe Utichi, "Stranger Things' Star Millie Bobby Brown Talks," *Deadline*, August 11, 2017.

24   "In *Stranger Things* this season…": Crystal Bell, "David Harbour Made Millie Bobby Brown Cry With His Critics' Choice Acceptance Speech," *MTV*, January 12, 2018.

25   "After the first season…": Genevieve Valentine, "Stranger Things' treatment of Barb reveals the show's greatest flaw: its limited view of women," *Vox*, August 3, 2016.

26   "Asked about the critique…": Melissa Leon, "Inside 'Stranger Things': The Duffer Bros. on How They Made the TV Hit of the Summer," *The Daily Beast*, August 7, 2016.

About the Author

Joseph Vogel is the author of several books, including *Man in the Music: The Creative Life and Work of Michael Jackson* and *This Thing Called Life: Prince, Race, Sex, Religion, and Music*. His work has been featured in *The Atlantic*, *Slate*, *The Guardian*, *Forbes*, and *The Huffington Post*. He is an Assistant Professor at Merrimack College in Massachusetts.

Made in United States
North Haven, CT
15 July 2022

21432768R00133